CAMBRIDGE

COMPACT

KEY
FOR SCHOOLS
SECOND EDITION

WITH
DOWNLOADABLE
RESOURCE PACK

A2

TEACHER'S BOOK

Emma Heyderman and Jessica Smith

For the revised exam from 2020

Cambridge University Press
www.cambridge.org/elt

Cambridge Assessment English
www.cambridgeenglish.org

Information on this title: www.cambridge.org/9781108348881

First published 2014
Second edition 2019

20 19 18 17 16 15 14 13 12 11 10 9 8 7 6 5 4

Printed in Great Britain by CPI Group (UK) Ltd, Croydon CR0 4YY

A catalogue record for this publication is available from the British Library

ISBN 978-1-108-34888-1 Teacher's Book with Downloadable Resource Pack

Contents

Map of the units

UNIT	TOPICS	GRAMMAR	VOCABULARY	FUNCTIONS
1 **My family, my friends & me**	Family People	*have got* Present simple Question words	Family Daily activities Describing people	Talking about routines and habits Asking for and telling the time Describing everyday activities
2 **In my free time**	Hobbies & leisure Personal opinion	Adverbs of frequency *Do you like …? / Would you like …?*	Free-time activities	Expressing preferences, likes and dislikes Giving and responding to invitations
3 **Eating in, eating out**	House & home Food & drink	*There is / are, a / an, some & any* *(don't) have to*	House & furniture Food & drink	Saying where things are Describing food Ordering food Expressing obligation
4 **What are you doing now?**	Sport Clothes	Present continuous Present continuous vs present simple	Sport Clothes	Talking about what people are doing now Describing what people are wearing
5 **Great places to visit**	Places & buildings Time	Past simple *ago* Time expressions: *in / at / on*	Places Days & dates	Describing places Talking about dates Talking about events in the past
6 **Getting there**	Transport Travel	Comparative adjectives Superlative adjectives	Transport	Making comparisons
7 **School rules!**	Education Entertainment	*must / mustn't* *should /shouldn't* *can / could* Adverbs of manner	Education Musical instruments	Expressing rules and obligation Giving advice Talking about ability in the present and past
8 **We had a great time!**	Holidays Personal experiences	Past continuous Past simple & past continuous	Holiday activities Adjectives of opinion	Talking about events in progress in the past Giving opinions
9 **What's on?**	Entertainment & media Television	*be going to* Infinitives & *-ing* forms	Going out TV programmes Word-building	Making suggestions Talking about future plans
10 **Are you an outdoors person?**	The natural world Weather	*will / won't & may* First conditional	The countryside Weather & seasons	Following instructions Making predictions about the future Expressing certainty and doubt
11 **Healthy body, healthy mind**	Health & medicine Personal feelings	Present perfect *just* *yet / already* Present perfect with *for & since*	The body Health & illness Adjectives	Talking about recent past events Talking about health problems Discussing personal feelings
12 **Technology & me**	Communication Appliances	The passive: present The passive: past simple	Communication & technology Describing objects	Describing simple objects Checking understanding

READING	WRITING	LISTENING	SPEAKING
Part 2: Three texts about family	Part 7: Story	Part 3: A conversation about a school day	Part 1: Describing people
Part 3: An interview with a teenage painter	Part 5: Completing an email about a boy's family, friends and hobbies	Part 4: Five short conversations	Part 1: Asking and answering about free time
Part 4: An article about a boy from Mali	Part 7: Story	Part 2: A talk about a school trip to a school of cooking	Part 2: Asking and answering about meals
Part 1: Notices and messages	Part 6: An email about clothes	Part 1: Five short conversations	Part 2: Asking and answering about clothes and fashion
Part 2: Three texts about a school trip	Part 6: An email about a shopping trip	Part 2: Information about a Hollywood tour	Part 1: Questions about things you did this week
Part 3: An article about a teenage inventor	Part 5: An email about a trip to San Francisco	Part 5: A conversation about getting to a birthday party	Part 2: Asking and answering about means of transport
Part 1: Notices	Part 6: An email about school	Part 2: A talk by a new teacher	Part 1: Questions about school subjects
Part 4: An article about a holiday in Guadeloupe	Part 7: Story	Part 5: A conversation about where friends stayed on holiday	Part 2: Asking and answering about holidays
Part 3: An article about a teenager's unusual life	Part 6: A message to a friend about a show	Part 4: Five short conversations	Part 1: Questions about plans for the evening and a holiday
Part 1: Notices and messages	Part 7: Story	Part 1: Five short conversations	Part 2: Asking and answering about outdoor activitie
Part 4: An article about the history of glasses Part 2: Three texts about staying in hospital	Part 6: An email about keeping fit	Part 3: A conversation about a Healthy Living Day	Part 1: Questions about yourself
Part 2: Three texts about teenagers and computers	Part 5: Completing emails about a lost phone	Part 5: A conversation about favourite things	Part 2: Asking and answering about technology

1 My family, my friends & me

UNIT OBJECTIVES

A2 KEY FOR SCHOOLS TOPICS: family, daily life, people

GRAMMAR: *have got*, present simple, question words

VOCABULARY: family, time, daily activities, describing people

READING AND WRITING PART 2: understanding the task; **PART 7:** describing pictures with correct prepositions

LISTENING PART 3: understanding the task

SPEAKING PART 1: answering the *tell me something about ...* question

Family

Grammar

Grammar – *have got*

> **STARTER**
> With books closed, write the question *Have you got an unusual family?* on the board. Invite a brief class discussion on what an unusual family might be, e.g. a lot of brothers and sisters, family members with the same names or birthdays.

1 Students open their books and do the exercise. Point out the definition under the text and make sure students understand the word *twin*.

> **Answers**
> 1 F (I've got a twin brother and we've got two sisters.)
> 2 T (I've got the same name as my dad and his dad.)
> 3 T (I've got the same birthday as my sister, my mum and her sister.)

2 Encourage the students to tell you when we use *have got* (with *I, you, we, they*) and *has got* (with *he, she, it*). Point out the use of contractions in Exercise 1 (*I've got, we've got*), and remind students that these are short forms of *I have got* and *we have got*.

> **Answers**   Words to underline:
> Title: Have you got
> Tim: Yes! I've got
> Mathilde: Yes, I have; I've got the same
> Emin: I've got a twin; we've got two sisters.
> Question 1: Emin hasn't got
> 1 We use *have* or *has* and *not*
> 2 We use *Have I/you/we/they got ...?* or *Has he/she/it got ...?*
> 3 We use the verb *have* without got (*Yes, I have. No, I haven't.*).

3 Point out that all the examples of mistakes in the 'correct the mistake' exercises in this book are taken from real A2 Key or Key for School exam scripts. Refer students to the Grammar reference on page 90. They can use these pages before or during the exercises. They can also use them to help them revise.

> **Answers**   1 she gots = she has got / she's got
> 2 she got = she has got / she's got
> 3 I'm got = I've got / I have got
> 4 my father gets = my father has got / my father's got

4 Encourage the students to read the whole text first before they start writing. Check they understand *nickname* by reading the definition under the exercise.

> **Answers**   2 Have ... got   3 haven't (have not)
> 4 've (have) got   5 's (has) got   6 hasn't (has not) got
> 7 've (have) got   8 have got

> **FURTHER PRACTICE**
> In pairs, students ask and answer questions about their names and their family and friends' names. Brainstorm a list of possible questions on to the board first, e.g. *Have you got an unusual name? Have your friends got nicknames? Has your brother got an unusual name?*

▶ *See the Workbook and online resources for further practice.*

People

Reading & Writing Part 2

1 With books closed, brainstorm a list of family words and write them on the board. Make sure the list includes the words needed in this exercise. Encourage the students to find male and female pairs of words, e.g. brother & sister, son & daughter.

With books open, ask the students to look at Sofia's family tree first. Ask and answer questions around the class about it, e.g. *Has Sofia got any brothers or sisters? What are Sofia's parents' names? Has she got any cousins?* Encourage the students to read Sophia's blog post first before they complete it. With a weaker class, read through the blog post as a class, stopping at each gap and eliciting the answer using the family tree.

> **Answers**   2 parents   3 aunt   4 uncle
> 5 children/daughters   6 cousins   7 grandfather   8 wife
> 9 sons

> **FURTHER PRACTICE**
> The students could draw their own family tree and then tell their partner about their family.

Sample answer
A boy bought a book in a shop. He left his wallet in the shop, and the shop assistant saw it. The shop assistant went out of the shop and returned the wallet to the boy. The boy was very happy.

☑ Exam task

Tell the students that in Reading & Writing Part 2, they read three short texts about different people, books, films, places, etc. They then match information with the correct text by answering seven questions.

Read through the questions as a class first and make sure that everyone understands them. This could be done by asking students around the class to answer the questions about themselves, e.g. *Who lives with a grandparent? Me. I live with my grandmother.*

Read the exam tip as a class. Students do the exam task. Encourage them to underline the information in the text which gives them the answer to each question.

Answers	1 C	2 A	3 B	4 C	5 C	6 B	7 A

Reading & Writing Part 7

1 Tell the students that in Reading & Writing Part 7, they have to write a story of 35 words or more based on three pictures.

With books closed, brainstorm the answer to the question *Where is your favourite place to spend time?* Write the students' answers on the board. After the students have completed the exercise, ask them if the places shown in the pictures are the same or different to the places they chose.

Answers	1 bedroom	2 park	3 beach	4 street
5 school				

2 Read the exam tip together and then ask students to complete the exercise using the correct preposition from the box. Make sure that the students understand that there are some extra prepositions in the box that they do not need to use.

Answers	1 in	2 to	3 on	4 along	5 out of

FURTHER PRACTICE
Students make sentences using the words on the board from Exercise 1 (their favourite places to spend time) and adding a preposition to talk about each one, e.g. *Yesterday I went to the sports centre.*

3 Look at the first picture as a class and read the sentence that describes it. Point out that the sentence is in the past simple. Ask students to suggest ideas to describe what happened in the following two pictures. Try to elicit the vocabulary required to describe the pictures: *shop assistant, wallet, return, happy.* Then ask students to write one or two sentences to tell the story. Check as a class and accept any stories which are appropriate.

☑ Exam task

Ask students to read the instructions and remind them that they have to write a story of 35 words or more based on three pictures. Contractions (e.g. *didn't*) count as two words (*did + not*).

Let students look at the three pictures for a few minutes in order to understand the story. Then ask them to write the story. Select three or four students to read their stories to the class. Accept any appropriate stories. Make sure students understand that there can be more than one correct answer.

Sample answer
When she woke up, Ana stayed in her bedroom and called her friend. She talked for a long time and arrived late at the breakfast table. Her dad got very angry and told her to eat quickly. Unfortunately she didn't finish in time and she missed the school bus.

Daily life

Grammar & Vocabulary

1 If necessary, revise the time in English by writing several examples on the board and asking students *What's the time?* Point out that they might hear different ways of asking the question (*What's the time?* or *What time is it?*) and telling the time (*It's seven forty.* or *It's twenty to eight.*) Point out that we don't usually use the 24-hour clock when telling the time, so we don't say *It's nineteen forty.*

Do the first time as a class, then ask students to work in pairs asking and answering the questions.

Answers
1 What's the time in 1? It's seven forty or twenty to eight.
2 What's the time in 2? It's nine thirty or half past nine.
3 What's the time in 3? It's twelve fifty-five or five to one.
4 What's the time in 4? It's three fifteen or a quarter past three.
5 What's the time in 5? It's ten forty-five or a quarter to eleven.
6 What's the time in 6? It's eleven thirty-five or twenty-five to twelve.

2 Students look at Kyle's photo album first to try to identify the verbs in the pictures before they read the expressions 1–8.

Answers	2 G	3 F	4 E	5 C	6 B	7 A	8 H

3 🔊 02 Before the students listen, they should try to predict what time Kyle does the things in the photos, e.g. *I think Kyle walks to school at 8.30. What about you?*

Answers	B 8.45	C 9.00	D 1.20 / 13.20	E 4.00 / 16.00
F 4.10 /16.10	G 8.00 / 20.00	H 9.30 / 21.30		

Recording script

Friend:	Tell me about what you do every day, Kyle.
Kyle:	Well, (A) I usually wake up at eight o'clock. I have a shower and I have breakfast. (B) I leave home at a quarter to nine and I walk to school with my friends. (C) School starts at nine o'clock and if we're late, the teacher gets angry.
Friend:	Really? Do you have lunch at school?
Kyle:	Yes, I do. (D) We have lunch at twenty past one.
Friend:	What do you do after school?
Kyle:	School finishes at three forty-five and (E) I get home at four o'clock. I usually have a snack like a piece of bread or some biscuits and then (F) I do my homework at about ten past four. We have dinner when my parents get home and then (G) at eight o'clock, we all watch TV together.
Friend:	What time do you go to bed?
Kyle:	My sister goes to bed at nine o'clock and (H) I go to bed at half past nine.

Grammar – the present simple

4 With books closed, ask the students questions about the present simple using the rules, e.g. *When do we add -s or -es to the main verb? How do we make the negative, questions and short answers?* If necessary, refer the students to the Grammar reference on page 90.

> **Answers**   1 c   2 a   3 b

5 Remind the students that there is only one mistake in each of these sentences.

> **Answers**   2 don't have = doesn't have
> 3 want = wants
> 4 do = does
> 5 What you think = What do you think
> 6 It doesnt matter = It doesn't matter

6 Do the first two sentences as a class. Point out that the times are probably not true for the students so they will need to write a sentence in both the negative and the affirmative, giving the correct information, e.g. *I don't wake up at 7.00. I wake up at 7.30.*

> **Sample answers**
> 2   I don't walk to school with my friends at 8.30. I catch the bus at 8.10.
> 3   School doesn't start at 9.00. It starts at 8.30.
> 4   I don't have lunch at 12.00. I have lunch at 1.00.
> 5   My friends don't do their homework at 4.00. They do their homework at 5.30.
> 6   My mum doesn't get home at 6.00. She gets home at 7.00.
> 7   We don't watch TV at 7.00. We watch TV at 8.30.
> 8   My best friend doesn't go to bed at 8.30. He goes to bed at 10.00.

▶ *See the Workbook and online resources for further practice.*

Listening Part 3

1 🔊 **03** Ask the students to read the instructions in the exam task and to tell you what they have to do in the task: listen to Simon talking about his school day and

choose the correct answer. Encourage the students to look at the picture and to say what is unusual about Simon's day. Read the exam tip as a class. Ask the students to work in pairs and take turns to read and say the times in Exercise 1 before they listen.

> **Answers**   1 a   2 a

Recording script

Amanda:	Hi, Simon! How are you?
Simon:	Oh hi, Amanda! I'm tired!
Amanda:	Me too! I go to sleep really late because my brother watches TV in his room, and I can hear it.
Simon:	Oh, that's a shame! But you don't have to get up really early, like I do!
Amanda:	Get up really early? Why's that?
Simon:	I take the boat to school now. It goes at half past seven, so (1) Mum wakes us up at a quarter past six. We have breakfast and (2) leave home at seven.

✅ Exam task

🔊 **04** Encourage the students to read through all the questions before they listen and to ask you for help with any words they don't understand. Point out that in the exam they will listen to each recording twice. Play the recording once. Students can help each other with any answers they didn't hear. Play the recording again. If you wish, photocopy the recording script on page 54 for each student. Ask them to underline the sentences which give them the answers. Play the recording again.

> **Answers**   1 B   2 C   3 B   4 A   5 C

Recording script

You will hear Simon talking to his friend Amanda about his school day.

Amanda:	Hi, Simon! How are you?
Simon:	Oh hi, Amanda! I'm tired!
Amanda:	Me too! (1) I go to sleep really late because my brother watches TV in his room, and I can hear it.
Simon:	Oh, that's a shame! But you don't have to get up really early, like I do!
Amanda:	Get up really early? Why's that?
Simon:	I take the boat to school now. (2) It goes at half past seven, so Mum wakes us up at a quarter past six. We have breakfast and leave home at seven.
Amanda:	So you've changed schools?
Simon:	Yes. The school on our island is for six to eleven year olds. (3) Now I'm twelve, I go to school on another island with my sister Tanya. She's fourteen now.
Amanda:	Oh. What about getting home?
Simon:	The boat goes two hours after school finishes. (4) Mum's sister lives near the school so we have dinner there.
Amanda:	So that's your school day! (5) It's not like mine – much more interesting – and longer!
Simon:	It's what everyone my age on the island does.
Amanda:	Some people probably think it's fun, or even exciting, but I don't like boats.
Simon:	Well, it's the only way!

CLIL Geography: In small groups, students choose four or five islands around Great Britain and research each one. They find out about the population and services, e.g. schools and shops. Students produce a short report on each of their chosen islands. As a class, they produce a large map of Great Britain and stick their reports near their chosen islands.

Grammar – Question words

2 With books closed, brainstorm the question words (*how, what, what time, when, where, who*) and write them on the board. Encourage the students to tell you when we use each one. If necessary, help the students by asking questions, e.g. *What word do we use to ask about a place? (Where) A time? (What time or When) A date? (When).*

> **Answers** 2 Where   3 What time   4 How   5 When   6 What

3 Check the students' answers and then encourage the students to ask and answer the questions in pairs. Play the recording again if necessary. Alternatively, divide the class into two or three teams and invite one student to come to the front to be the quizmaster. All the other students close their books. The quizmaster asks the questions and the teams have to answer them correctly in full sentences.

> **Answers** 1 a   2 a   3 a   4 b   5 b   6 a

4 Explain that to write the questions, students have to choose one word or phrase from each box. As a class, make two or three questions together. If necessary, remind the students how to form present simple questions and that we use *do* with *I, you, we, they* and *does* with *he, she, it*. In pairs, students take turns to ask and answer their questions.

> **Sample answers**
> Who is your best friend? What do you do in the evening? Where do you go to school? How do you go to school? What time does your brother wake up? When does your mum go to work?

People

Speaking Part 1 (Phase 2)

1 Revise vocabulary to describe people (e.g. *curly/straight, long/short, dark/fair + hair; tall/short; brown/green/blue eyes*). With a stronger class, encourage the students to describe the people in the picture before they read the sentences.

> **Answers** 2 A   3 D   4 C

FURTHER PRACTICE
Students write descriptions of people they know, e.g. their teacher, best friend.

---

2 Begin by giving the class an example. Describe someone in the room, perhaps yourself, and encourage the students to say who it is. Check students' work as they write their sentences in pairs.

3 Students work in groups of six so each group has to listen to three descriptions. They follow the example and use the question and answer *Is it …? Yes, it is. / No, it isn't.* Fast finishers continue by describing some famous people.

4 🔊 **05** Point out that there are two parts in the Speaking exam, and that each part has two phases. In Part 1 Phase 1, the examiner asks each candidate some personal questions. Then, in Part 1 Phase 2, the examiner asks a *Tell me something about …* question about the candidate's daily life and interests.

> **Answers** 1 your English teacher   2 your school day

> **Recording script**
> Examiner: Ana, tell me something about (1) your English teacher.
> Ana: Mrs Reed.
> Examiner: Malik, tell me something about (2) your school day.
> Malik: Well, I wake up at a quarter past eight. I walk to school with my friends. School starts at nine o'clock. After school, I do my homework and then I watch TV.

5 Read the exam tip as a class. Point out that students should speak using full sentences where possible.

> **Answers** Malik gives the best answer because he speaks in full sentences and he says more than Ana.

6 Elicit from the class that Ana doesn't give a good answer because 'Mrs Reed' isn't a full sentence and Ana doesn't answer with at least three sentences.

> **Sample answers** 2 She's got short, dark hair and blue eyes.   3 She goes to school by car.   4 She doesn't have lunch at school.   5 I like her because she's very nice.

✓ Exam task

Students work in pairs. Give them time to think about their answers before they do the task. Remind them to use full sentences and answer with at least three sentences.

> **Sample answers**
> 1 A: Tell me something about your school day.
>   B: I wake up at 7.30. I go to school with my dad. School starts at 8.30. After school, I walk home and then I do my homework.
> 2 A: Tell me something about your favourite teacher.
>   B: Her name's Mrs Reed. She's got short, dark hair and blue eyes. She goes to school by car. I like her because she's very nice.
> 3 A: Tell me something about what you do at the weekend.
>   B: I wake up at 9.00. I play football with my friends or we ride our bikes. On Sunday, I go to my grandparents' house.
> 4 A: Tell me something about your best friend.
>   B: His name is Lucas. He's got short, dark hair and blue eyes. He's quite tall. I like him because he's very funny.

2 In my free time

Hobbies & leisure

Grammar & Vocabulary

STARTER
With books closed, brainstorm a list of activities that the students do in their free time. Use the question *What do you do in your free time?* Try to elicit some of the activities that are in the book, e.g. *watch films, play sports.*

1 Ask the students to work in pairs to complete the activities with the verbs. Remind them to use each verb only once.

Answers
2 collect things
3 play sports
4 draw pictures
5 take photos
6 watch films
7 listen to songs
8 sleep in a tent

2 Encourage the students to read the whole message first before they complete it. Point out that these are all examples of verb + noun combinations / collocations and it is a good idea to learn these words as chunks, rather than as separate words, e.g. *take photos* rather than *take* and *photos*.

Answers 1 photos 2 films 3 in a tent 4 to songs
5 instrument 6 pictures

Grammar – Adverbs of frequency

3 Check that students know what an adverb of frequency is first. Elicit some examples. Point out that it might be

a short word like *usually* or *sometimes* or it might be a longer expression like *once a month*. Refer students to the Grammar reference on page 92.

Answers
1 after 2 before 3 both answers correct

4 Ask students to read the whole text first and then try to find the mistakes. Point out that they may be spelling mistakes, word order mistakes or a word which needs changing. Students check answers in pairs before checking as a class.

Answers
2 normaly = normally
3 often are = are often
4 somtimes = sometimes
5 I don't never eat = I never eat / I don't ever eat
6 ussually = usually
7 two times a month = twice a month
8 Always she cooks = She always cooks

5 Point out that the students need to read the complete sentence first before they choose the word.

Answers 2 three times a week 3 every day 4 always

CLIL Maths – using graphs: Students work in groups. Each group chooses a different hobby or free-time activity and designs a class survey about it using *How often do you ...? or Do you ever ...?* This could be an oral survey or the students could use a free online survey tool like Survey Monkey to create a written survey. Students then ask everyone in the class to respond to their survey and make a graph of the results. The graph could be a bar graph or a pie chart. Each group presents their results to the rest of the class.

▶ *See the Workbook and online resources for further practice.*

Listening Part 4

1 Point out that there are five parts in the Listening paper and that these exercises look at Part 4. Ask students to work in pairs to find the answers to the questions by looking at the exam task.

Answers
1   five
2   three
3   Question 2 – 1 person
    Question 3 – 2 people
    Question 4 – 2 people
    Question 5 – 1 person

2 🔊 **06** Ask students to read the extracts from the conversation before they listen. Tell them to try to think of a word which might go in each gap. Make sure students understand that these are extracts and the recording includes other information too. Tell them that

Jasmine is the first speaker and Abbey is the second speaker. Play the recording and repeat if necessary.

| Answers | 1 also | 2 reason | 3 haven't |

Recording script

Jasmine:	I saw a film yesterday. That actor you like was in it. He's really good-looking, isn't he?
Abbey:	Yes, he is. He's also a really good actor. That's the reason I prefer him to any other actor.
Jasmine:	Mm. Maybe the film I saw yesterday wasn't one of his best!
Abbey:	Yeah, in the last few years his films haven't been very good.

3 Read the exam tip as a class and go over the instructions. Ask students to work in pairs to underline the parts of the conversation which mention A, B and C. Emphasise that they are looking for where the speakers mention, and not necessarily agree with, each option – the speakers might disagree with an option, e.g. A. Check answers as a class.

Answers
A 'In the last few years his films haven't been very good.'
B 'He's really good looking, isn't he?' 'Yes, he is.'
C 'He's also a really good actor. That's the reason I prefer him to any other actor.'

4 Read the instructions together as a class and see if the students can identify which answer is correct and why. Highlight how important it is for students to understand the precise meaning of the question.

Answer The right answer is C, because Abbey says 'That's the reason I prefer him to any other actor.'

☑ Exam task

🔊 07 Encourage the students to read the exam task. Make sure they understand all the vocabulary. Ask them to name an example of each type of film in 1 to check understanding (*comedy* is a false friend in some languages). Play the recording twice.

You can photocopy the recording script on page 54 for each student. They listen again and underline the sentences that give the answers.

| Answers | 1 B | 2 C | 3 C | 4 A | 5 B |

Recording script

1 You will hear two friends talking about a film they've just seen. What type of film was it?

Boy:	I really liked that film.
Girl:	Me too! Usually I prefer adventure stories, and I've never liked scary films before, but that one was great – really enjoyable.
Boy:	I know! It's strange, isn't it, that we think it's fun to be frightened.

| Girl: | Yeah, that's funny, isn't it? But we only like it when we know it's not real. |

2 You will hear a boy talking about a camping trip. Who did he go camping with?

We had a great time camping. The weather was good, so my uncle and I cooked outside every day. His cooking isn't as good as my mum's, but it's OK. Because it was sunny during the day, it was still quite warm at night, too. I'm lucky – I've never been camping when it's rainy. My brother has. He says it's awful!

3 You will hear a boy, James, talking to his mother about basketball lessons. What does James ask his mother to do?

Mum:	Did you see the information about your basketball lessons, James?
James:	Yeah – thanks for booking those, Mum. I read the information so I know when the lessons start.
Mum:	Yes – next week! Do you need new T-shirts and shorts?
James:	Mm. I have some shorts, but they're a bit tight. Can you get me some new ones?
Mum:	Yes, I'll do that tomorrow.

4 You will hear two friends discussing a practice for their dance group. What do they still need to do?

Boy:	Is everything ready for dance practice tomorrow?
Girl:	Nearly. I've downloaded a video of the dance we chose on my phone.
Boy:	Great! We picked a good one! Mr. Davies has agreed that we can use the hall, so we have somewhere to dance.
Girl:	Good. One more thing – I'm not sure if everyone knows what time to come.
Boy:	OK. I'll send a message.

5 You will hear a girl talking about horse riding. Why does she like horse riding?

I started horse riding last year. I didn't really know anything about horses before, but my friend goes riding, and she invited me to go with her. I go regularly now. It's really fun. It's great to be out in the countryside, in the fresh air – much better than being in a sports centre.

Grammar

Grammar – *Do you like ...? / Would you like ...?*

1 In pairs, students read the dialogue together. Ask which question we use to ask someone if they like something (*Do you like + -ing?*) and which question we use to invite someone to do something (*Would you like + infinitive?*).

Sample answers
Sam loves eating food from all over the world but he doesn't want to join Ruby's club. He isn't interested in cooking.

2 Encourage the students to read the conversations with gaps all the way through first before they complete them. Refer students to the Grammar reference on page 92.

Answers
2 Do you like reading   3 Would you like to come
4 Would you like to go   5 Do you like playing
6 Would you like to watch

3 With books closed, invite different students to do things and ask for a response, e.g. *Would you like to go to the cinema? No. Would you like to play a game? Yes.* Point out that short answers like *yes* and *no* sound rude in English and brainstorm some longer replies, e.g. *Yes, please. No, thanks.* Write these on the board.

> **Answers**
> Underline: I'd love to Circle: (I'm afraid not.) / (Not really.)

4 If you wrote possible replies on the board in Exercise 3 (see above), encourage the students to compare their ideas with the expressions in the book.

> **Answers**
> Yes: I'd love to., That's great – thanks!, Sure!, Good idea.
> No: No, thanks, I'm afraid not., I'm sorry, I can't., I'm afraid I'm busy., I'd like to, but I can't.

5 Check that the students understand the events by asking them which sound the most/least interesting. Model the first conversation in the example with a strong student. Encourage fast finishers to make up some more dialogues.

> **Sample answers**
> A: Would you like to run a 5km-run this summer?
> B: I'm afraid not. I can't run fast.
> A: Would you like to go camping this weekend?
> B: I'm sorry, I can't. I'm busy this weekend.
> A: Would you like to visit the Science Museum tomorrow?
> B: Good idea! I love that museum.

▶ *See the Workbook and online resources for further practice.*

Reading & Writing Part 3

1 Encourage the students to look at the exam task and say what they have to do in Reading & Writing Part 3 (read a text and choose the correct option from three choices for five questions). Make sure the students understand that they may need to look for synonyms of the words in the text when choosing the correct answer. Tell them that synonyms are words that mean the same. The students match the words that mean the same, then check their answers in pairs.

> **Answers**   1 e   2 d   3 b   4 a   5 f   6 c

2 Read the question and the three possible answers together as a class and check understanding. Then students read the text. Point out that the part of the text which is underlined is where they can find information about answer B. Explain that although the boy says that the author's stories aren't easy to understand (i.e. they are difficult), he doesn't say that the book is too difficult for him to finish, so answer B is wrong. The students do the exercise, then talk in pairs about which answer (A or C) is correct. Check as a class.

> **Answers**   A – she's not well-known
> C – I hope no one tells me how it ends
> The correct answer is C.

☑ Exam task

Ask the students to read the introduction to the interview. Then ask some questions to check understanding, e.g. *How old is Kris?* (15) *What does he do?* (he paints / he has a website of his own paintings). Ask students to read the questions first. Point out that the answers to questions 1–4 are in the same order in the text. The final question is a global question, referring to the text as a whole.

> **Answers**   1 C   2 B   3 B   4 C   5 A

Personal opinions

Speaking Part 1 (Phase 2)

1 Explain that in Speaking Part 1 there are two phases. In Phase 1, candidates answer factual personal questions about their name, age and where they come from or live. In Phase 2, they answer three questions about daily life, interests, likes, etc. The first two questions are short-answer questions (though responses should not be too short) and the third is longer, *Tell me something about ... .*

Go over the expressions in the box with the class. Ask the students to say which expressions have the stronger negative or positive meaning; i.e. *hate / be terrible at, be brilliant at / love.*

> **Answers**
> **Positive:**   enjoy   prefer   love   like   be brilliant at
>   be interested in
> **Negative:**   don't like   be terrible at   be bad at

2 Go over the example with the class. Point out that after all these expressions, we use the *-ing* form. Also point out that the students can use the activities in the box or their own ideas.

> **Sample answers**
> 2 playing computer games, cooking
> 3 going to concerts, dancing
> 4 messaging friends, reading books
> 5 trying new food, cooking

3 Remind the students that the question here is *Do you like + -ing?* Encourage the students to answer with a variety of the opinion expressions.

> **Sample answers**
> Do you like playing computer games? Yes, I do. I'm good at playing computer games.
> Do you like going to concerts? Yes, I do. I'm interested in going to concerts.
> Do you like reading books? Yes, I do. I enjoy reading books.
> Do you like trying new food? No, I don't. I hate trying new food.

4 Remind the students that in Speaking Part 1 Phase 2, the examiner will ask personal information questions, e.g. about their free-time activities. Point out that the conversation here shows the examiner asking short-answer questions at the beginning of Phase 2. In pairs, students read and complete the conversation, writing down the missing words. Don't check them yet.

> **Answers** 1 Do you play   2 do you spend

5 🔊 **08** Play the recording for students to check their answers. Then ask students *Are the candidate's answers good or not?* (They're not good because they are rather short.) Encourage the students to think of ways they could improve the candidate's answers.

> **Recording script**
> Examiner: Now, let's talk about weekends. What sports do you play at the weekend?
> Candidate: I'm sorry, I don't understand.
> Examiner: (1) <u>Do you play</u> football at the weekend?
> Candidate: No. I play volleyball.
> Examiner: Who (2) <u>do you spend</u> time with at the weekend?
> Candidate: I spend time with my friends.

6 Elicit ideas from the class before they read the example.

> **Sample answers**
> I usually have a volleyball match with my team on Saturday or Sunday morning. We play at the sports centre.
> I always spend time with my friends at the weekend. Sometimes I go shopping with my friends on Saturday afternoon.

✓ Exam task

Point out that the examiner asks three questions in the conversation only because the candidate does not understand the first question. Therefore, Student A should only need to ask two questions: *What sports do you play at the weekend?* and *Who do you spend time with at the weekend?* Remind Student B to use the opinion expressions (*I love, enjoy, prefer,* etc.) on the page and adverbs of frequency. Encourage the students to take turns to be student A and B.

> **Sample answers**
> I sometimes play football in the park on Saturday afternoon.
> I usually go swimming on Sunday morning.
> I usually see my friends on Saturday morning. Sometimes we go to the town centre. I spend Sunday with my family.

▶ *See the Workbook and online resources for further practice.*

1 Encourage the students to look at the exam task and say what they have to do in Reading & Writing Part 5 (read a text such as an email or message and add six missing words). Point out that if they write more than one word, the answer is not correct. Read the exam tip as a class.

> **Answers** 2 it   3 him   4 her   5 we   6 she   7 them   8 it

2 Elicit one or two sentences from the class first to check that everyone knows what to do. Encourage them to use pronouns in their answers. Either correct any mistakes with pronouns when the students make them or write a list of their mistakes on the board for them to correct when they have finished speaking.

> **Sample answers**
> He's got a camera so he likes taking photos with it. I think he enjoys drawing because there's a picture. He plays the drums because there are drums in the picture. I think he likes adventure films because there's a poster on the wall and music because of the headphones. He likes reading because there are some books above the bed.

3 Encourage the students to read the email first without writing, pointing out that it is good exam technique to read through the text first to get a general idea. Ask some general questions to check that the students have understood the email, e.g. *Where is Hasan from? Has he got any brothers or sisters?*

> **Sample answers**
> In his free time, Hasan likes listening to music. He plays the drums and he goes to the cinema. He sometimes has dinner in a pizza restaurant.

✓ Exam task

Stress that the students can write **one** word only. They should check they have used the correct pronouns in 2 and 5.

> **Answers** 1 have/'ve   2 Their   3 to   4 a   5 we   6 about

> **FURTHER PRACTICE**
> Students can use Hasan's email to help them write their own message about themselves.

> **Sample answer**
> My name is Alejandre but my friends call me Alex. I'm 12 years old and I live in São Paulo, Brazil. I've got two brothers. Their names are Enzo and Vitor.
> In my free time, I like watching films. On Saturdays, I always meet my friends and we go to the cinema. I also enjoy taking photos with my camera.

3 Eating in, eating out

UNIT OBJECTIVES

A2 KEY FOR SCHOOLS TOPICS: house & home, food & drink

GRAMMAR: *there is/are, a/an, some & any, (don't) have to*

VOCABULARY: house & furniture, food & drink

READING & WRITING PART 4: using context to choose answers;. **PART 7:** using correct tenses

LISTENING PART 2: writing prices in pounds (£) correctly

SPEAKING PART 2: answering questions about likes and dislikes

House & home

Grammar & Vocabulary

STARTER
With books closed, ask the question *Which rooms do you have in your house?* Brainstorm the names of different rooms. Then ask students to name one piece of furniture they have in each room.

1 In pairs, ask the students to look at the pictures and to say what time of day it is and where the people are in each picture (A bedroom; B living room; C hall; D bathroom; E kitchen). If necessary, point out that Harun is a boy's name.

> **Answers** 2 E   3 B   4 A

2 Encourage the students to think of some more items to add to the table. Ask the students if they can find the items in the table in the pictures in Exercise 1.

> **Sample answers**
> **bedroom:**   desk, lamp, mirror, shelf, chair
> **bathroom:**   toilet, shower, mirror
> **living room:** bookshelf, sofa, mirror, chair
> **kitchen:**   cooker, cupboard, fridge, shelf, chair

Grammar – *There is / are, a / an, some & any*

3 You could do this exercise as a memory test. Ask the students to look at the pictures for one or two minutes and then close their books. Read the sentences and elicit the answers. When the students have finished, ask them to underline examples of *There is* and *There are* and *a/an, some* and *any* and to say when we use each one. If necessary, refer the students to the Grammar reference on page 93.

> **Answers** 2 Angela   3 Harun   4 Noelia

4 Ask the students to say why the words are wrong, e.g. question 1: we usually use *some* in positive sentences and requests and not *any*; question 2: we use *an* before a vowel sound.

> **Answers**
> 2 a assistant chef = an assistant chef
> 3 is there a sofa = there is a sofa / there's a sofa
> 4 some money = any money
> 5 a beautiful trainers = some beautiful trainers
> 6 there are a small bed = there is a small bed / there's a small bed
> 7 there is a lot of different things = there are a lot of different things

Reading & Writing Part 4

1 With books closed, ask the students if they know which ingredients are needed to make an omelette. Write their suggestions on the board and try to elicit some of the food vocabulary from the text message conversation, e.g. eggs, salt, butter. Remind students to read the conversation all the way through before doing the exercise.

> **Answers**   Underline: make, break, mix, cook, cut up, add

2 It may be helpful to ask students to say what they can use to do the actions described by the verbs, e.g. *you cut with a knife, you mix with a spoon.*

> **Sample answers**
> You use the instructions to make an omelette.
> You break an egg to use it.
> When you mix, you put two things together.
> You cook the egg before you eat it.
> You cut something up into small pieces.

3 Read the exam tip as a class. Point out that the students should try to understand each option before deciding which one is the correct answer.

4 Ask the students to do the task in pairs. Make sure they talk about each option.

> **Answers**   1 A   2 B   3 B   4 C

✓ Exam task

Encourage the students to read the instructions and to say what they have to do in this part (read a text and choose the best word). Ask the students to read the complete text including the title first without writing. Then with books closed, they tell you what they learned about Moussa. With books open, focus the students' attention on the first two gaps and ask them what words are missing. The students then complete the rest of the task individually.

FURTHER PRACTICE

In pairs, students ask and answer questions about what they have for breakfast and who they eat with; e.g. *What do you have for breakfast? Do you have it with your parents?*

[CLIL] Geography – Students work in small groups and use the internet to find out more about the country of Mali. Each group should produce a poster, giving information about the country, e.g. population, national flag, climate, culture, food.

▶ *See the Workbook and online resources for further practice.*

Food & drink

Grammar & Vocabulary

1 With books closed, brainstorm a list of food and drink onto the board. With books open, students try to find the words on the board in the pictures. Elicit other kinds of food and drink they can see. Tell students to read the complete descriptions before they start writing. Clear up any problems with vocabulary.

Answers 2 milk 3 fish 4 rice 5 soup 6 onions
7 chicken 8 juice

2 The students match the descriptions with the pictures. Check answers.

Answers 2 Picture C 3 Picture A

FURTHER PRACTICE

In pairs, the students ask and answer questions about the food they like, e.g. *Do you like chicken and fish? I like chicken but I don't like fish very much.*

Grammar – (don't) have to

3 Point out that many schools in the UK, Australia, South Africa and New Zealand have a 'tuck shop' which sells food, drink and often stationery, too.

Answers 1 fast food like burgers and pizza 2 at school / in his classroom

4 Students read the interview again and underline the answers in the text. Point out that we use *(don't) have to* to talk about things which are and aren't necessary.

Answers
2 T (I have to pay for my lunch before school starts.)
3 F (Two students have to collect our food from the tuck shop.)
4 F (We don't have to wash up.)

5 Check that the students know how to write the positive, negative and question form of *have to* first. If necessary, refer the students to the Grammar reference on page 93.

Remind students to read the conversation before writing.

Answers
2 Do; have to wake up
3 have to get up
4 Do; have to tidy
5 don't have to tidy
6 have to make
7 has to make
8 have to eat

FURTHER PRACTICE

In pairs, students ask and answer questions about things they have to do at home, e.g. *Do you have to wash up? Do you have to clean the floor? Do you have to tidy your room?*

[CLIL] Geography/Cooking: Students work in small groups. Each group chooses a different country and researches the national dish of that country. They should produce a list of ingredients and a recipe.

▶ *See the Workbook and online resources for further practice.*

Listening Part 2

1 🔊 [09] Ask the students to look at the picture and predict what the recording is about (buying something in a fast food café). Read the exam tip together. Tell students if they need to complete a price in Listening Part 2, this price will always be in pounds (£). Check they know how to write prices in pounds (£) and that we use a dot '.' to separate the pounds from the pence (£5.56). Then, write some prices on the board and make sure students know how to pronounce them, e.g. £3.50 = three pounds fifty / £1.40 = one pound forty / 35p = thirty-five p. Tell students that the answers are in the same order as the questions. If necessary, play the recording several times.

Answers 2 £2.80 3 89p 4 £1.15 5 £1.35

Recording script

Server:	Next customer, please!
Boy:	Oh, that's me!
Server:	Can I help you?
Boy:	Yes. Can I have a fried egg, please?
Server:	One or two eggs?
Boy:	One egg, please. How much is it?
Server:	(1) That's one pound seventy-five. Do you want bread and butter with that?
Boy:	Yes, please. No, wait. How much is an omelette?
Server:	That's two pounds twenty-seven or (2) two pounds eighty with cheese.
Boy:	OK. I'll have a cheese omelette and a slice of bread and butter, please.
Server:	Anything to drink?
Boy:	How much is a cup of hot chocolate?
Server:	(3) All our hot drinks are eighty-nine p. And how about a piece of cake, too?

Boy: Oh. OK. How much is it all?

Server: So, a cheese omelette, (4) <u>a slice of bread and butter for one pound fifteen</u>, a cup of hot chocolate and (5) <u>a piece of our special cake for one pound thirty-five</u>. That's six pounds nineteen.

Boy: Here you are.

Server: Enjoy your meal!

FURTHER PRACTICE

In pairs, students ask and answer questions about the prices on the menu, e.g. *How much is the fried egg? It's £1.75.* Check that students know how to say the prices correctly before they begin.

2 Help the students if necessary by writing question prompts on the board, e.g. 1 How / get there? 2 What time / at school? 3 bring / anything special? 4 learn / to cook there?

> **Sample answers**
> 1 How can we get there?
> 2 What time do we have to be at school?
> 3 Do we have to bring anything special?
> 4 Can we learn to cook there?

3 After students have read through the exam task, ask them to say what information is missing in each gap, e.g. 1 name, 2 transport, 3 time, 4 cooked item, 5 price.

> **Answers** Questions relating to name, transport, time, food and price are likely to be correct.

☑ Exam task

◁)) **10** Play the recording at least twice. If you play it more than twice, remind students that in the exam they will hear each recording twice only.

> **Answers** 1 Stice 2 bus 3 8.15 / eight fifteen 4 cakes
> 5 9.50 / nine fifty

> **Recording script**
> *You will hear a teacher telling students about a school trip.*
>
> Teacher: Right everyone, I want to tell you about the trip to the school of cooking next week – on the 16th of February. Some of you have asked me which school of cooking we're going to – well, (1) <u>it's called Stice – you spell that S-T-I-C-E</u>. Some of you may know it – it's in town, near the train station. We won't be going by train, but (2) <u>by bus</u>. It's easier to keep everyone together that way. Now, on the day of the trip, you'll have to get to school earlier than usual, as our trip starts at nine o'clock. (3) <u>Please be here at 8.15</u>. Don't be late! It's a school of cooking, so we'll be making something. The group I took last year made pizzas, which were fantastic, and I'm sure (4) <u>the cakes we make this time</u> will be just as good. (5) <u>Tell your parents that they'll need to pay nine pounds fifty for the day</u> – that includes five pounds for the food that we're going to make. Good, that's everything.

FURTHER PRACTICE

Ask students to tell you which of the questions in Exercise 2 they can now answer.

4 Remind the students that they might be asked about the food they eat in Speaking Part 1. Encourage the students to answer in complete sentences. If necessary, model a good answer first.

> **Sample answers**
> 1 I like chicken and chips. I also like eggs and omelettes.
> 2 I usually have lunch at my grandmother's house.
> 3 My mum and my dad cook in my house. Yes, I do. I have to put the plates on the table. I also have to clean the table when we finish.

Speaking Part 2 (Phase 2)

1 Point out that in Speaking Part 2, there are two phases. In Phase 1, students have a discussion with the other candidate about the activities or objects shown in some black and white pictures. In Phase 2, the examiner asks the candidates two more questions on the same topic.

Read the exam tip as a class and make sure the students understand that they have to talk about some pictures in Speaking Part 2 Phase 1. Tell the students that they should give reasons for their answers in the exam. Ask them to do the exercise in pairs, but don't check their answers yet.

2 ◁)) **11** Tell the students that they are going to hear six conversations which include the answers to Exercise 1. Play the recording twice if necessary.

> **Answers** 1 f 2 e 3 a 4 b 5 d 6 c

> **Recording script**
> 1
> Boy: Do you like strawberries, Carla?
> Carla: Yes, (1) <u>I like strawberries because they're fresh and sweet</u>. I like them more than any other fruit.
> 2
> Girl: Do you like burgers?
> Boy: No. (2) <u>I don't like fast food because it's not good for your health</u>. I prefer salads.
> 3
> Girl: Do you like the food in your school canteen?
> Boy: (3) <u>I never eat in my school canteen because the food there isn't very good</u>.
> 4
> Girl: Do you like breakfast, Marco?
> Marco: Yes, (4) <u>I love breakfast, because I'm always hungry when I wake up</u>! I have a really big breakfast.
> 5
> Boy: Do you like going out to eat with your family, Erika?
> Erika: Yes, (5) <u>I like going to restaurants because I can try new kinds of food</u> – things that my mum doesn't cook at home.

6

Boy: Do you enjoy cooking, Suzanna?

Suzanna: Yes, (6) I enjoy cooking because it's fun to learn new things. And it doesn't really matter if you make a mistake. You can just start again!

3 🔊 **12** Ask the students to look at the pictures and name some of the things they can see, e.g. eggs, chips. Students listen to the recording and decide which candidate gives the best answer. Encourage them to give reasons for their answer. Point out that in the exam, there will be five pictures (or six pictures if there is a group of three candidates).

> **Answer**   The girl, because she gives reasons.

> **Recording script**
> Girl: Do you like cooking?
> Boy: No, I don't. Do you like fast food?
> Girl: No, because it has lots of sugar and other things that are not healthy. Do you like sandwiches?
> Boy: Not really.

4 Remind the students to give reasons for their answers. Ask two or three pairs to have a conversation in front of the class. Ask the other students to decide whether they think the pairs give good answers (by giving reasons).

✓ Exam task

Look at the pictures as a class and brainstorm some useful vocabulary (restaurant, kitchen, living room, café, barbecue, burger, chicken leg, salad, coffee, etc.). Then ask the students to work in pairs to do the task. When they have finished, you could ask the students why they like or don't like eating in the different places to see how many ideas the class can generate.

> **Sample answers**
> I love eating at a restaurant with my family or friends. My favourite food is Chinese.
> I like eating at my grandmother's house because she cooks my favourite dish.
> I enjoy having a barbecue with my friends in the summer. We listen to music while we eat.
> I like eating my lunch while I watch TV. It's fun.
> I don't like eating in a café because the food isn't very good.

Reading & Writing Part 7

1 Ask the students if they remember (from Unit 1) what they have to do in Reading & Writing Part 7 (write a story of 35 words or more based on three pictures). Check that students understand the phrases. After the students have completed the task, ask them to compare their answers in pairs.

> **Answers**

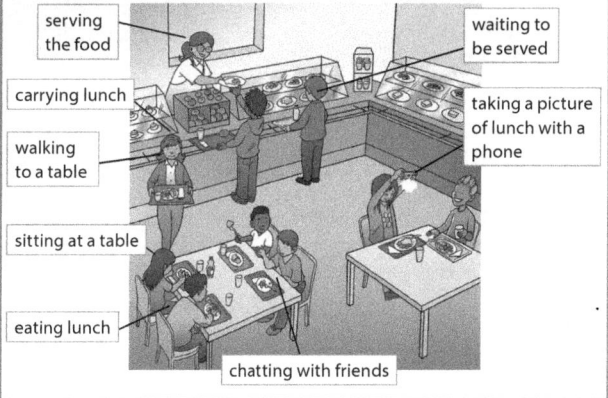

2 Remind the students that some of the verbs are irregular.

> **Answers**
> walked, sat, carried, ate, took, served, waited, chatted.

> **Sample answers**
> A woman served the food.
> Two students waited to be served.
> Some students chatted and ate their lunch.
> A student took a photo of her lunch with her phone.

3 Go over the exam tip as a class. Point out that some of the verbs in the sentences are spelled correctly, but there is one verb which is not spelled correctly in each sentence.

> **Answers**
> 1 stoped = stopped
> 2 singed = sang
> 3 payed = paid
> 4 visitted = visited

4 Brainstorm some vocabulary for the pictures. Remind the students of the food words they looked at earlier which could be useful here (eggs, butter, mix, bowl, biscuits). Students work in pairs. After they have written their sentences, ask some pairs to read their stories to the class.

> **Sample answer**
> A boy is in the kitchen. He is mixing eggs, butter and other things in a bowl. Now he is taking the biscuits out of the oven. They look delicious!

✓ Exam task

Ask students to do the task individually, reminding them again of the information in the exam tip.

> **Sample answer**
> There was a party in the garden. Dad cooked food on the barbecue. Then it started to rain. Everyone ran into the house. They took all the food and furniture. Dad cooked the food in the cooker, and everyone was happy again.

5 Point out that the students need to check their work in the exam, too. Encourage them to count the words in their story. Tell them to remember to write more than 35 words, but no more than the word limit of 65 words. Ask them to check their partner's story after checking their own.

4 What are you doing now?

UNIT OBJECTIVES

A2 KEY FOR SCHOOLS TOPICS: sport, clothes

GRAMMAR: present continuous, present continuous vs. present simple

VOCABULARY: sport, clothes

LISTENING PART1 / READING & WRITING PART 1: understanding the task and underlining key words

READING & WRITING PART 6: understanding the task

SPEAKING PART 2: talking about clothes

Sport

Grammar & Vocabulary

STARTER
Give students five minutes working in small groups to write down as many different sports as they can. Compare lists.

1 Explain what 'tips' (useful suggestions) are. Give students five minutes working in pairs to do the exercise. Check answers.

> **Answers**   swimming 6   ice hockey 4   table tennis 3
> fishing 2   basketball 5

FURTHER PRACTICE
Create a table on the board with the class and encourage the students to keep a record of the new sports in the unit:

Sport	Equipment
skateboarding, table tennis	skateboard, bat, ball

2 Elicit from the class which sports are used with *play* (ball sports), *go (-ing)* and *do* (other sports). Encourage the students to add more sports to the table. Use the ones in Exercise 1 to begin with (go fishing/skateboarding/ swimming; play basketball / table tennis / ice hockey). If you have created a Sports Table in Exercise 1 (see above), insert a *play/go/do* column before 'sport'.

> **Answers**   play: basketball, table tennis, ice hockey, football, golf
> go: fishing, skateboarding, swimming, cycling, skiing, ice-skating, surfing
> do: aerobics, athletics, martial arts

FURTHER PRACTICE
In pairs, students ask and answer questions about the sports they do, e.g. *What sports do you do? How often do you do them? Where do you do the sports?*

Grammar – Present continuous

3 Read the text as a class and check the answer to the question (tennis). Elicit the words that tell them the sport is tennis; i.e. *a racket, small yellow balls, hit a ball, win 40–15.* Students underline the examples of the present continuous in the text and say when we use it (an activity which is happening now) and how we form it (*be (not) + -ing*).

4 Students try to correct the spelling mistakes. Then they compare their corrections with the spelling rules of the *-ing* form in the Grammar reference on page 94.

> **Answers**   2 wating = waiting   3 styding = studying
> 4 workin = working   5 lisening = listening
> 6 cooming = coming

5 Remind students about short answers to present continuous questions (*Yes, it is. / No, he isn't,* etc.) by asking some questions. For example: *Is your mum working at the moment? (Yes, she is. / No, she isn't.) Is Mario eating now? (Yes, he is. / No, he isn't.)* Tell students to read the conversation before writing.

> **Answers**   2 'm (am) watching   3 Is the school team winning   4 is   5 's (is) playing   6 Is Toby sitting   7 isn't   8 's (is) buying   9 're (are) losing

▶ *See the Workbook and online resources for further practice.*

Listening Part 1

1 Look at the exam questions in Exercise 2 and the exam task together as a class. Say that in the exam, there are five questions to answer in Listening Part 1. Here, the five questions are split across Exercise 2 and the exam task.

Ask the students to look at the instructions for the exam task and work in pairs to complete the sentences in Exercise 1.

> **Answers**   1 five   2 one   3 three

2 Read the exam tip as a class. Tell students to read the question carefully. Then look at the pictures and decide how each one answers the question. Underlining the important words and thinking about each picture will help them to focus on the correct information in the listening.

> **Answers**   1 What's Cara <u>doing</u> <u>now</u>?   2 A She's swimming
> B She's mountain biking C She's climbing

3 🔊 **13** If necessary, play the recording twice.

Answer	C

Recording script

1 *What's Cara doing now?*

Boy: Cara wasn't at swimming practice today. Is she ill?
Girl: No, she's fine. She's in the mountains with her family.
Boy: Really? Is she mountain biking again?
Girl: No, she's learning to climb. She's got a great teacher.

4 🔊 **13** Remind the students that they will hear information about all three pictures but only one piece of information will answer the question on the exam paper correctly.

Answers	1 C 2 A 3 B

✓ Exam task

🔊 **14** Before they listen, encourage the students to read the questions and underline the important words. They should also look at the three pictures for each question and think about how the pictures answer each question, e.g.:

2 How much is Jenny's new tennis racket?
A It's £35 B It's £40 C It's £45.
3 What time does the hockey match start?
A At 4.10 B At 4.20 C At 4.30
4 What is Simon drinking?
A lemonade B orange juice C hot chocolate
5 Who is Maisie's table tennis coach?
A He's got blond hair and glasses. B He's got dark hair.
C He's got dark hair and glasses.

Point out that in the exam, students should think about the differences between the three pictures before they listen.

After the students have completed the task, hand out photocopies of the recording script on page 55. Ask the students to underline the correct answer and circle the other items in the pictures that are mentioned.

Answers	2 B 3 C 4 A 5 B

Recording script

2 *How much was Jenny's new tennis racket?*

Boy: I love your new tennis shoes, Jenny. Were they expensive?
Girl: No, they weren't. They were £35. My racket was more expensive.
Boy: Oh really? How much was that?
Girl: (2) I bought it online for £40. My sister paid £45 for hers.

3 *What time does the hockey match start?*

Girl: Excuse me. What time does the hockey match start?
Man: (3) It starts at half past four.
Girl: What time is it now? Am I late?
Man: No, it's only ten past four. Go for a walk and come back at twenty past four.

4 *What is the boy drinking?*

Girl: I'm thirsty after that race.
Simon: (4) This lemonade is really good. I bought it over there in the café.
Girl: Is there any juice?
Simon: I don't think so, but they've got hot chocolate if you prefer that.

5 *Who is the girl's table tennis coach?*

Maisie: That's my table tennis coach.
Boy: Who? Is he that blond man over there with glasses?
Maisie: No, (5) he's got dark hair and he doesn't wear glasses.
Boy: Oh, I can see him now. He's standing over there next to Brendan.

Clothes

Grammar & Vocabulary

1 Pre-teach *wheelchair*. Encourage the students to answer in complete sentences, e.g. *I think he plays basketball because ...*

Answers	1 basketball 2 football 3 swimming

2 Read through the clothes as a class. Check that the students understand each word and can pronounce them correctly. Encourage the students to ask complete questions (*What's she wearing?*) and answer in full sentences (*She's wearing ...*).

Sample answers
1 He's wearing a basketball shirt, some trousers and trainers.
2 She's wearing shorts, a T-shirt, some socks and and some boots.
3 She's wearing a swimming costume.

Grammar – Present continuous vs. present simple

3 After matching the texts, in pairs students guess the meanings of some of the vocabulary from context; e.g. *team, competition, train, race* and *medal*.

Answers	a 2 b 3 c 1

4 Check that the students can identify the present simple and present continuous by finding the first example of each tense together as a class. Refer the students to the Grammar reference on page 94.

Answers
PC: she's getting ready; She's feeling excited; He's preparing
PS: plays; trains; has to; is; swims; goes; swims; 's got; hopes; comes; loves; say; 's; wants

5 Ask the students questions to see how much they know before they do this exercise, e.g. *Do we use the present simple or continuous to talk about the things we do every day? And the things which are happening now?* Also elicit the time adverbs we use with each one; *e.g. now, at the moment, today, this week* with the present continuous; *often, usually, every day, twice a week* with the present simple.

6 Do this exercise in stages. First, ask the students to look at the picture and identify the sport (baseball). Then, students read the whole text without writing. Ask them to think about which verb goes in which gap. Next they should look for words which tell them if it is the simple (*usually*) or continuous (*at the moment*). With a weaker class, first read the complete text to the class with the verbs in their correct form.

Answers   2 plays   3 trains   4 're (are) thinking
5 's (is) getting   6 wants

CLIL Sport: In small groups, students choose a country in another part of the world and find out information about a sport in that country which isn't normally played in the students' own country. Students should find information about the equipment needed, the clothes and the rules. The groups present their sport to the class using pictures and diagrams. You could give suggestions, e.g. Spain (*padel*); Italy (*bocce*), Southeast Asia (*sepak takraw*), China (*wushu*), Finland (*pesäpallo*), South Africa (*jukskei*).

▶ *See the Workbook and online resources for further practice.*

Reading & Writing Part 1

1 Ask the students to look at the exam task and answer the questions in pairs. Check answers as a class. Remind students that in the real exam there are six questions to answer, but in the exam task here there are only five.

Answers   1 a message or notice 2 three

2 Read the exam tip together as a class. Point out that understanding why the writer wrote the message or notice will help the students identify the correct answer. Ask the students to read the message from Ethan, choose the correct answer and underline the part of the message that gives the answer.

Answer
A – I'm going cycling on Saturday. Are you interested?

3 Ask students to work individually or in pairs to complete the exercise. Allow them to compare their answers before checking as a class.

Answers
1 a member of staff   2 I can be there by 2 p.m.
3 Sale ends tomorrow.

4 Ask the students to identify the differences between messages and notices. Establish that messages usually include the names of the writer and the recipient. Ask students if they can see any examples of notices in the classroom. What information do the classroom notices communicate? Students do the exercise in pairs. Check answers.

Answers
1 message: text message / short message on social media
2 notice: sports centre / swimming pool
3 message: text message / short message on social media
4 notice: shop
5 notice: school / sports centre

✓ Exam task

Ask the students to do the task individually. Check answers together as a class. While checking answers, ask the students which parts of the messages helped them identify the correct answers.

Answers
1 A - Shall we pick you up?
2 C - The pool temperature is lower this week
3 B - Can you look for it?
4 B - 50% off all swimming costumes
5 A - come to the sports field for practice, this evening only

FURTHER PRACTICE
For fast finishers or more able students, ask them to work in pairs to write a message or short notice. Then they exchange their message or notice with another pair, who say why the message or notice was written.

Reading & Writing Part 6

1 Point out that in Reading & Writing Part 6, students read some instructions or a short text and write a short email, note or message in response. Students' responses have to cover three points/questions given in the instructions or text. Students must write 25 words or more.

Students read the instructions and the email, then answer the questions.

Answers
1 An email to Alice.
2 three: Where do you want to meet? What time do you want to meet? What are you going to wear?
3 25 words or more

2 Remind the students of what makes a good answer (writing over 25 words and answering all three questions). Encourage the students to justify their choice of best answer and also say why the other two answers are not good.

Answer   2 is the best answer because it answers the three questions and it is over 25 words.

3 Before students read the teacher's comments, encourage them to think of what a teacher might write for each one.

Answers   a 3   b 1   c 2

✓ Exam task

Read the exam tip as a class. Ask the students to answer the three questions in Exercise 1 about this exam task

(1 an email to Ed; 2 three questions: What do you usually wear for school? What are your favourite kinds of clothes? How often do you go clothes shopping?; 3 25 words or more). Let students have eight minutes to write the email. When counting the words, include all parts of the email – the opening and closing as well as the main body. Also, contractions such as *I'm* count as two words (*I am*).

> **Sample answer**
> Hi Ed,
> We can wear what we like for school. My favourite clothes are jeans, jumpers and T-shirts. I go clothes shopping about six times a year.
> See you soon,
> Michele

4 Before collecting in the students' writing, make sure they check their work by answering the questions in the exercise.

Speaking Part 2 (Phase 2)

1 Brainstorm what the students remember about Speaking Part 2 (there are two phases: in Phase 1, students have a discussion with the other candidate about the activities or objects shown in some black and white pictures; in Phase 2, the examiner asks each candidate two more questions on the same topic). Then ask the students what the general topic of the pictures is. Point out that by the time they get to Phase 2, the pictures will have been taken away from them; the pictures are used here to introduce the topic (clothes/fashion). Ask the students to do the exercise in pairs. Then compare answers as a class.

> **Sample answers**
> He's wearing a tracksuit and trainers, and he's wearing jeans, a shirt and shoes.
> He's wearing a suit / a jacket and trousers.
> She's wearing a dress and boots.

2 Students read the three questions, then work in pairs to match each question to a picture. Check answers.

> **Answers** 1 B 2 C 3 A

3 🔊 **15** Ask the students to think about what a good answer would be like. For example, it would be more than one or two words long and would include reasons/explanations. Go over the exam tip as a class. Students listen to the recording and discuss their answers in pairs.

> **Answer** The boy's answers are the best. He uses longer sentences, doesn't repeat exactly what the examiner says, gives reasons for his answers, and uses adjectives to compare.

> **Recording script**
> Examiner: Do you prefer wearing sport clothes or jeans?
> Girl: Jeans.
> Examiner: Why?
> Girl: I don't play sport.
> Examiner: And what about you?

> Boy: I like sports clothes more than jeans because they're more comfortable. And I wear trainers a lot.
> Examiner: Do you spend a lot of time deciding what to wear?
> Boy: Not really. I just put on what's clean!
> Examiner: And you?
> Girl: Yes, I spend a lot of time deciding what to wear.
> Examiner: Why?
> Girl: I don't know.
> Examiner: Are you interested in fashion?
> Girl: Yes, I love fashion.
> Examiner: Why?
> Girl: I just love it.
> Examiner: And what about you?
> Boy: No, I'm not really interested in fashion. I prefer to spend my time playing sport, or going out with my friends.
> Examiner: Thank you.

FURTHER PRACTICE
Play the recording again and ask the students to make a note of the girl's and boy's answers to the questions. Students compare their notes in pairs and then talk about how the boy's answers are a good example of the exam tip.

4 Tell the students that the adjectives in the box can be useful when talking about clothes. Students complete the sentences and then compare their answers with a partner. Point out the difference between *fun* (enjoyable) and *funny* (humorous/comical), which are commonly confused. Encourage students to write other forms of the adjectives used in the exercise in their vocabulary notebooks, e.g. *bright, cheap, pretty*. With stronger students, you could ask them for the opposite of the words used in the sentences (and/or synonyms).

> **Answers** 1 comfortable 2 warm 3 fun 4 cheaper
> 5 prettier 6 brighter

5 Remind the students to give complete answers including reasons. Encourage them to use some of the adjectives from Exercise 4.

✓ Exam task

Students work in pairs to ask and answer the questions. In the exam, students will answer two questions in two minutes. If appropriate, you could introduce some expressions, such as *I agree / I don't agree* and encourage students to extend their answers using *and, but* or *because*. Encourage students to ask their partner 'Why?' if necessary, but point out that in the exam, students are not expected to interact with each other in Part 2 Phase 2.

FURTHER PRACTICE
Ask two or three pairs to role-play the questions and answers in front of the class. The other students listen and decide which pair gives the best answer to each question and why.

UNIT OBJECTIVES

A2 KEY FOR SCHOOLS TOPICS: places & buildings, time

GRAMMAR: past simple positive, negative and questions, *ago*, time expressions *in/at/on*

VOCABULARY: places & building, days & dates

READING & WRITING PART 2: answering negative questions; **PART 6:** starting and finishing well

LISTENING PART 2: writing dates, times and numbers correctly

SPEAKING PART 1: answering questions about the past, saying when with *in, at, on* + time expression

Places & buildings

Grammar & Vocabulary

STARTER

Have a brief class discussion on the places in the students' town using the words in the box in Exercise 1 and these questions: *Have you got these places in your town? What places do tourists usually visit? Where do you usually go with your friends/family?*

1 Go over the words in the box. Check students' pronunciation. Students complete the sentences in pairs.

> **Answers**
> 2 museum   3 department store   4 theatre*   5 police station
> 6 bookshop   7 university   8 pharmacy

*In the UK, it is common to eat ice cream during the interval at the theatre.

CLIL Geography: Students work in pairs to draw a map of the area immediately around their school. They should mark shops, cinemas, the school, etc., using symbols. Each group should then present their map to the class. The whole class takes a vote on the best map.

Grammar – Past simple positive

2 Encourage the students to look for clues, e.g. a *capital city in Europe, he went to the National Museum of Scotland*.

> **Answer**   He's in Edinburgh, Scotland.

3 If necessary, explain that we form regular verbs in the past by adding -ed to the verb. Other verbs are irregular and students need to learn these. (There is a

list of irregular verbs at the back of their book). Remind students that the past simple form of *be* is *was* or *were*.

> **Answers**   Underline: explored, stopped, enjoyed, studied
> Circle: got, had, was, went

4 Encourage the students to use the list of irregular verbs at the back of their books and the spelling rules of regular verbs in the Grammar reference on page 95 to help them do this exercise. Point out that the most common mistake is the past form of *cost*.

Point out that *traveled* in 3 is not correct in British English, but would be correct in American English. In the exam, students are not penalised for using American English but they need to use it consistently and cannot mix British and American spelling or usage.

> **Answers** 1 enjoed = enjoyed   2 costed = cost
> 3 traveled = travelled   4 lefted = left

5 Students read the complete text before writing. Refer them to the list of irregular verbs and the Grammar reference on page 96 to check the past simple forms. Check spelling.

> **Answers**   1 was   2 died   3 moved   4 found   5 was
> 6 decided   7 began   8 wrote   9 needed   10 tried
> 11 were   12 opened

▶ *See the Workbook and online resources for further practice.*

Reading & Writing Part 2

Grammar – Past simple negative

1 Use the sentences in the exercise or alternatively, with books closed, write some false sentences on the board, e.g. *Levi Strauss was born in the USA* and ask the students to correct the sentences using the past simple negative.

> **Answers**   1 wasn't, weren't   2 didn't + infinitive

2 Ask the students to identify the tenses used in the questions in the exam task (1 and 3 use the present simple, 2, 4 and 5 use the past simple). Then ask them to find the verb in the past simple negative. Go over the exam tip to point out the significance of the negative verb in the question (it means that the information in the text may be positive).

> **Answers**   Question 4 in the exam task is negative (Who didn't like …).

3 Students do the exercise in pairs. Go over their answers as a class.

> **Answers**   1 didn't enjoy   2 didn't have   3 didn't go
> 4 didn't see   5 didn't arrive   6 wasn't

4 Try to elicit the difference between a fact and an opinion (a fact is always true; an opinion depends on what someone thinks).

> **Answers** In Exercise 3, questions 1 and 6 are asking about opinions.

5 Students read the texts to identify the opinion each person has of the school trip. Students discuss in pairs who enjoyed the trip. Encourage them to give reasons for their answer.

> **Answer** Freddie

☑ Exam task

Point out that in the exam there will be seven questions to answer but here there are only five. Read the instructions together. Tell students to read the questions first and then read each text. Remind students that it may be possible to exclude wrong answers before they choose the correct answer to each question.

> **Answers** 1 C   2 B   3 A   4 B   5 C

FURTHER PRACTICE

Students write a short text in the past simple about an imaginary school trip to a castle using the texts in the exam task as a model. Tell students to include answers to some, but not all, of the questions in the exam task in their text. In groups of three or four, the students take turns to read out their texts. Then, ask the questions in the exam task, remembering to include masculine forms where necessary. The students reply with the names of students whose stories included answers to the questions, e.g.:

Who is happy with the photos she or he took at the castle? Jean, Maria

Who found out something which surprised him or her? Ana, Markus

Time

1&2 Encourage students to make a guess at the answers using *I think it's … because …* Ask the pair(s) of students with the most correct answers where they'd like to go for their prize – remind them it has to be a capital city.

> **Answers** 1 A   2 B   3 A   4 A   5 C

3 If necessary, revise the spelling and pronunciation of days, months and dates in English. Remind students that although we say 'Wednesday the fifth of March', we usually write Wednesday 5th March without *the* or *of*. We can also say 'March the fifth'. Tell students that after the year 2000 (two thousand) we changed the

pronunciation of the years and tend to say 'two thousand and four', although 'twenty oh four' is also possible. From 2010 we returned to the regular way of pronouncing years (twenty ten).

> **Answers** March the thirty-first; Wednesday the fifth; the twentieth of August two thousand and seven; July nineteen ninety-eight; Tuesday the third of February, twenty nineteen

Grammar – Past simple questions

4 Refer students to the Grammar reference on page 95.

> **Answers** 1 (Question word) + *was/were* + *I, you, he, etc.*
> 2 (Question word) + *did* + *I, you, he*, etc. + infinitive

5 Explain these sentences should be questions in the past simple. Students ask and answer in pairs.

> **Answers** 2 Did you enjoyed = Did you enjoy
> 3 Why you not come = Why didn't you come
> 4 What have you done = What did you do
> 5 How you know = How did you know

Grammar – *ago* & the past simple

6 Write two or three true sentences about yourself on the board, e.g. *I started working in this school* **a/one year ago.***; I went to New York* **six months ago.***; I saw a good film at the cinema* **three days ago**. Then ask the students questions to check they understand the meaning of *ago*, e.g. *When did I start working here? (last year) When did I go to New York? (last September). What word do we use to tell us when something happened? (ago) Do we write it before or after the time? (after)* The students will need to look at their quiz answers in Exercise 1 again to do this exercise. Refer students to the Grammar reference on page 95.

> **Answers**
> 1 two/2   2 23   3 96   4 110
> 5 100 (these answers are true for 2018)
> We use *ago* e.g. two centuries ago, 23 years ago, 96 months ago.

7 Point out that the students need to use the past simple + *ago* to say when they did it.

> **Sample answer**s
> I went shopping in a department store two weeks ago.
> I played sport in a sports centre two days ago.
> I saw a film at the cinema a week ago.
> I bought something in an online shop a month ago.
> I borrowed a book from the library three weeks ago.

FURTHER PRACTICE

In pairs, students ask and answer questions about their sentences with follow-up questions, e.g. *When did you last go shopping in a department store? I went shopping in a department store two weeks ago. (Where? What did you buy?) When did you last play sport in a sports centre? I played sport in a sports centre two days ago. (What sport did you play? Did you win?).*

▶ *See the Workbook and online resources for further practice.*

Listening Part 2

1 Focus on the photos and ask the students to say where they were taken (Hollywood). Invite a brief discussion on what the students know about Hollywood, e.g. films are made there so many film stars live there, the Oscar ceremony is held there. Point out the American spellings *theater* and *center*.

> **Answers** 1 Hollywood, California, USA.
> 2 The Dolby Theater is also a cinema; Lucky Devils is a restaurant; Hollywood Boulevard is a street; Staples Center is a sports stadium.

2 Ask students some questions about Listening Part 2, e.g. *How many people do you listen to in this part?* (one), *What do you need to complete?* (some notes with information), *What kinds of words do you need to write?* (places, days, dates, prices, numbers, etc.) (there may be one word which is spelled out). Then ask them to look at the exam task and to tell you what this task is about (a tour for young people).

> **Sample answers** 2 Address: 25, 709
> 3 Type of food: fast food, pizza 4 a sport: football, basketball
> 5 Price: $10, $20

3 🔊 16 Point out that the students have to spell the days and months correctly. Encourage the students to predict possible answers before they listen. Point out that for each question they will hear two possible days, dates, numbers, etc., but only one is correct. With a stronger class, play the recording again and encourage the students to listen for the other word and to tell you what it refers to. (1 9th = Selena left for Los Angeles, 2 Monday = they left on Monday evening, 3 Friday = they did a Hollywood tour, 4 two = she started school two days ago.)

> **Answers** 1 5th 2 Tuesday 3 Saturday 4 four

> **Recording script**
> (1) My birthday was on 5th April but we didn't leave for Los Angeles until 9th April. I remember the day well. We left on Monday evening and (2) we got there on Tuesday morning. The flight took about 11 hours. We were tired on the first day so we didn't do very much. We went on a Hollywood Tour on Friday but (3) the best day was Saturday because we saw the LA Lakers play a basketball match at Staples Center. (4) We got back four days ago and I started school again two days ago.

✓ Exam task

🔊 17 Read the exam tip as a class. If appropriate, point out that the price in this listening is in dollars ($). However, in the real exam, the price is always in pounds (£). Play the recording at least twice. Encourage the students to compare their answers in pairs before you tell them the correct ones.

> **Answers** 1 23rd July / July 23rd 2 (office at) 6000
> 3 burgers 4 basketball 5 27

> **Recording script**
> *For each question, write the correct answer in each gap. Write one word or a number or date or a time. You will hear some information about a tour for young people.*
>
> Our Hollywood tour for young people is called *Hollywood Living.* Join us for an exciting day (1) on July 23rd. We also have an adult tour on July 25th. To join the tour, please (2) be at our office at 6000 Hollywood Boulevard, ten minutes before the start. Hollywood Boulevard is home to some famous Hollywood cinemas – what we in America call movie theaters. We'll visit the Dolby Theater at 6801 Hollywood Boulevard and the Chinese Theater next to it.
>
> After that it will be time for lunch and (3) we'll go to Lucky Devils Restaurant for burgers. We might see somebody famous there, but most of the stars prefer to eat salads and other healthy food in Beverly Hills.
>
> In the afternoon, (4) we'll take a tour of the stadium where California's best basketball team plays, and you'll watch one of their games. Sorry, we don't have tickets for baseball or football games.
>
> This young person's tour costs (5) $27 for under 16s, and $37 dollars for any adults that come along too. Book your place now!

4&5 Ask the students to read the competition questions again and tell them that they should model their own questions on these. If necessary, write two or three questions together as a class. If appropriate, set up Exercise 5 as a class competition or a quiz show. Divide the class into teams; the teams take turns to ask their questions and answer the other teams' questions. Award 1 point for a correct question and 1 point for a correct answer.

> **Sample questions and answers**
> 1 When did the department store first open?
> A 2004 B 2010 C 2014
> 2 What did the footballer buy when he visited the store?
> A a football B some shoes C a shirt
> 3 When did the pizza restaurant open?
> A April 2018 B May 2018 C June 2018

CLIL Geography: In small groups, students plan a tour of their own town for tourists. Each group should think of a date for the tour, a place to meet, somewhere to have lunch, a place to go in the afternoon and the price. Then they should prepare a short description of their tour with a map. Each group takes turns to read their tour description. The others listen and write down the key information, i.e. the date, meeting place, lunch, afternoon visit and price.

CLIL History: Students work in small groups. Each group should choose a building in their local town (a different place from the one they may have chosen in Exercises 4 and 5). The students should use the internet to research the history of the building and write up this information in the form of a leaflet for visitors to the building. The groups then present their information to the rest of the class, who write down the key information and ask questions.

Reading & Writing Part 6

1 Have a brief classroom discussion on shopping using these questions: *1 Do you like shopping? Why (not)? 2 What kinds of things do you enjoy buying? 3 Did you buy anything last weekend? What did you buy?* Then brainstorm a list of different kinds of shops. Encourage the students to justify their answers, e.g. *I think they went to a clothes shop because I can see some new clothes.*

Sample answers They went to a clothes shop (clothes), a bookshop (books), a chemist (toothbrush, toothpaste & shampoo), a supermarket (food), a sports shop (tennis racket and balls), a DVD shop (DVDs), a newsagent (a newspaper), the post office (a parcel).

2 Encourage the students to justify their answer.

Sample answer I think she's feeling a little angry because she waited for her friend but she didn't come.

3 Ask the students to think of a suitable reply to Berta's email before they read the answers.

Answer 2 is better because it starts and finishes well.

4 Read the exam tip as a class. Ask the students to close their books and then think of ways they can start and finish a note or email. Students open their books and check their ideas.

Answers Starting: Hello; Dear John
Finishing: See you soon; Bye for now

✓ Exam task

Ask the class to read the exam task. Encourage the students to say what the difference is between this Part 6 task and the Part 6 exam task in Unit 4 Reading & Writing. (Here the students are told what to write in bullet points whereas in Unit 4 they have to answer an email or message. In both tasks however, they need to answer three questions or content points and write 25 words or more.) The students then answer these questions: *How can you start and finish this email? (Hi Zoe, Bye for now) What three pieces of information do you need to include? (Who you went shopping with, what you bought and what you did afterwards.) What words or expressions from this unit can you use? (go shopping, take the lift, department store, etc.).*

Sample answer Hi Zoe,
I went shopping with my cousin yesterday. We had a great time in the department store. I bought some new jeans. Afterwards, we took the lift to the sixth floor and we had a drink in the café.
Bye for now,
Kath

5 Remind the students that they should always check their work carefully before they finish.

Speaking Part 1 (Phase 2)

Grammar – Time expressions: *in/at/on*

1 With books closed, begin this section by writing two questions on the board: *Where did you go last weekend? What did you do?* In pairs, students take turns to ask and answer the questions. They then work in the same pairs to answer the questions in the exercise.

Answers 1 She went to Singapore.
2 She visited the science museum, she went shopping and they explored the Bird Park.

2 Ask the students to underline the examples of *in, at* or *on* with a time expression in the blog.

Answers 1 on   2 in   3 at   4 on

FURTHER PRACTICE
Read out these time expressions and ask the students for the correct preposition: *7 March, the weekend, 2011, 26 May 1999, the evening, October, 10.45.*

3 Elicit some questions as a class. Do not answer the questions now; the students will do this in the exam task.

Sample answers 1 Where did you eat on Tuesday?
2 Where did you go in the evening?
3 What did you do at 6.30 p.m. yesterday?
4 When did you eat on Tuesday?

4 🔊 **18** Point out that the examiner may sometimes ask questions about the past in Part 1 Phase 2. (In Part 2, the candidates usually ask and answer questions in the present.) Play the recording and remind the students they will have to justify their answers, e.g. *I think the girl/boy (doesn't) answer(s) the question well because …*

Answers The girl answers the questions well because she uses complete sentences in the past simple.
The boy doesn't answer well. He answers with words and not complete sentences.

Recording script
1

Examiner:	What did you do yesterday after school?
Girl:	I went to the sports centre.
Examiner:	What did you have for dinner?
Girl:	We had soup and bread.
Examiner:	What time did you go to bed?
Girl:	I went to bed at ten o'clock.
Examiner:	Thank you.

2

Examiner:	What did you do yesterday after school?
Boy:	Go library, do homework.
Examiner:	What did you have for dinner?
Boy:	Pasta.
Examiner:	What time did you go to bed?
Boy:	Ten o'clock.
Examiner:	Thank you.

5 Read the exam tip as a class. Remind the students that the examiner is asking questions about yesterday so the boy's answers need to be in the past.

Answers 2 I had pasta for dinner.   3 I went to bed at ten o'clock.

✓ Exam task

Encourage the pairs to take turns to be Student A and Student B. Remind Student A to ask questions about the past and Student B to answer using the past and *in, at* and *or*. Point out that in the exam each candidate will be asked two questions only.

Sample answers
A: Where did you eat on Tuesday?
B: I ate at home with my family on Tuesday.
A: Where did you go in the evening?
B: I went home and I did my homework in the evening.
A: What did you do at 6.30 p.m. yesterday?
B: I finished my homework and then we had dinner at 8 o'clock.

UNIT OBJECTIVES

A2 KEY FOR SCHOOLS TOPICS: transport, travel

GRAMMAR: comparative & superlative adjectives

VOCABULARY: transport, travel

READING & WRITING PART 3: guessing the meaning of a word from its context; **PART 5:** thinking of words that go together

LISTENING PART 5: understanding the task

SPEAKING PART 2: giving reasons for your answer

Transport

Grammar & Vocabulary

STARTER
With books closed, brainstorm forms of transport and write them on the board.

1 The words in the Sample answers below are the transport words on the A2 Key for Schools Vocabulary list. (This list is published by Cambridge Assessment English as a guide to the vocabulary needed to prepare students for the exam. It can be downloaded for free from the Cambridge English website – www.cambridgeenglish.org.)

> **Sample answers**   Sea: boat
> Land: lorry, tram, train, motorbike, bike, bus, car, coach, taxi, underground; Air: (aero)/(air)plane, helicopter

2 Ask the students to think about the types of transport we use with these verbs first, e.g. *drive + car, lorry and bus; sail + boat, ship, ride + bike.*

> **Answers**   2 fly   3 walk   4 ride   5 sail   6 cycle/ride

Grammar – Comparative adjectives

3 Tell the students that all the adjectives have to be changed to the comparative form to complete the sentences. Encourage them to work in pairs and make a guess if they are not sure of the answers. Then check answers as a class. Ask students some questions to check their understanding of the rules for using comparative adjectives. For example: *What do we add to short adjectives to make the comparative form? (-er) What word do we add before longer adjectives? (more) What other word do we use with comparative adjectives? (than) Do we use it before or after the adjective? (after).*

> **Answers**   1 busier   2 bigger   3 further/farther
> 4 more expensive   5 noisier   6 faster

4 Ask the students to look at the spelling rules for comparative adjectives in the Grammar reference on page 97 before they do this exercise.

> **Answers**   2 biger = bigger   3 yunnger = younger
> 4 more safer = safer   5 the more new = the newer

5 Encourage the students to read the complete text before they start writing. Check that the students spell the comparative adjectives correctly.

> **Answers**   2 faster   3 more expensive   4 bigger
> 5 more modern   6 cheaper   7 healthier (or more healthy)

FURTHER PRACTICE
In pairs, students write about transport in their town.

▶ *See the Workbook and online resources for further practice.*

CLIL History: Students work in groups. Each group chooses a form of transport (car, bus, train, plane) and uses the internet to find out what they can about the first examples of that form of transport. Students should then compare the original and modern forms of their chosen method of transport (e.g. modern cars are faster). Each group should present their information to the rest of the class.

Listening Part 5

1 Refer students to the exam task. This is the first time they have seen this type of task in this book so make sure they understand what they have to do (Listen to identify specific information – in this case, the form of transport used by each person – from a list). Then ask students to look at the picture. Point out that we say *go by train, bus, car, etc.* but *go on foot.*

> **Answers**   How did B get to the cinema? She went by bus, she didn't go by bike.
> How did C get to the cinema? She went on foot, she didn't go by bike.

2 🔊 **19** Read the exam tip as a class. Point out that the students will hear both answers, A & B, in this exercise but only one of them is correct. If necessary, play the recording twice. With a stronger class, ask the students to say if the correct answer is the first or second expression they hear.

> **Answers**   1 B   2 B   3 A

Recording script

Mum:	Did you have a good time at the cinema?
Yolanda:	Yeah, but my friends were late. Kathy missed the bus so (1) she went on foot.
Mum:	Really? What about Lisa? Did she walk too?
Yolanda:	No, she had lunch late so (2) she borrowed her brother's bike.
Mum:	And Sofia? She's always early.
Yolanda:	Not this time. (3) She took the bus. I told her it was quicker to cycle but she didn't listen.

3 Point out that the students need to write the answers on the pictures. Play the recording again if necessary.

Answers	A Lisa B Sofia C Kathy

☑ Exam task

🔊 **20** Ask the students to read through the lists of people (1–5) and transport (A–H) first. Encourage the students to think about what verbs they are likely to hear with each transport word, e.g. *go by train* or *bus*, *ride a bike*. After completing the task, hand out photocopies of the recording script on page 55. Students underline the correct answers.

Answers	1 C 2 H 3 E 4 A 5 F

Recording script

You will hear Ethan and his mum talking about his birthday party. How will each person travel to the party?

Ethan:	I'm home!
Mum:	Hi, Ethan! I'm in the kitchen. Happy Birthday!
Ethan:	Thanks, Mum! But where is everybody? Why are they so late for my party?
Mum:	Well, your sister has football practice until 6.00 p.m. (0) Then she's coming home by bus.
Ethan:	Why doesn't she take the tram? It's faster. And where's Dad?
Mum:	He phoned to say Grandma missed the half past five bus so (1) he's going to drive her.
Ethan:	Is Granddad coming in Dad's car, too?
Mum:	He had to work this afternoon (2) so he's going to take the underground. It's quicker than the car, anyway.
Ethan:	I can hear a motorbike. Is that Uncle Tom?
Mum:	I spoke to him this morning. (3) He's going to take a taxi after his meeting.
Ethan:	Is Ursula coming with him? Or is she taking the underground?
Mum:	(4) Your cousin Ursula's cycling here right now. She'll be here in ten minutes.
Ethan:	Great! Who else is coming?
Mum:	Your Aunt May!
Ethan:	Oh. She'll come by train, won't she?
Mum:	Actually, (5) there's a tram where she lives now, so she's getting that. It's nearer than the train.
Ethan:	OK. I hope they all get here soon!

4 Encourage the students to answer with complete sentences and to say why.

Sample answers How do you go to sports practice? My friend's dad sometimes drives us because it's faster than going by bus. When the weather's good, we go by bike because it's healthier.
How do you go to your friend's house? I usually walk because he lives very near and so it's quicker than going by car.
How do you go to the town centre? I usually go by bus. Sometimes my mother drives me.

Reading & Writing Part 3

1 Read the exam tip as a class. Ask the students to do the exercise in pairs.

Answers	*Crowded* means full of people. The parts of the text that help are 'someone sitting in every seat' and 'a lot of people standing up'.

2 Ask the students to read the whole text first without worrying about the underlined words. Then encourage them to read around each underlined word to try to understand the meaning. Students compare their answers in pairs.

Answers weighed – was very heavy
delay – when something starts later than it should
passenger – a person who is travelling on a plane, boat, car, etc, but isn't driving it
frightened – afraid or worried
lost – no one knows where it is

3 Make sure the students understand the exercise by doing number 1 together as a class. Then ask them to complete 2–6 in pairs.

Answers	1 B 2 C 3 B 4 A 5 A 6 C

4 The exam task should be approached in stages. First, work as a class to elicit answers to 1 a and b. Then, read 2 a and b and point out that the explanation for the word *invent* is in the description under the picture. Point out that it is important that students look at all the information around the text, not just the text itself. Finally, ask students to read question 1 in the exam task and then work through 3 in Exercise 4 together checking understanding at each stage as follows:

First, ask students to underline the sentence in the first paragraph of the text which includes the word *grandfather* (*When she was younger she spent time with her grandfather, who made transport for people to go into space*). Then ask students 'Is option C correct?' (the information is correct but it does not answer the question). Then, ask students to underline the sentence which includes the word *competition* (*Alexis often enters competitions for young inventors*). Ask students *Is option A correct?* (No – we know she often enters competitions but not that she wanted to win a specific competition). Then students underline the sentence which includes the word *mother* (*One day Alexis' mother told her about a newspaper article…. hospital in Africa*). Ask students

Does this sentence tell us the answer to the question?
(Not completely – we need to continue reading). Read
question 3b as a class and point out that the final
sentence in the paragraph helps to identify the correct
answer.

> **Answers**
> 1
> a) Sample answers; a girl, a new type of transport, carrying
>   something heavy, pulling something
> b) to give information
> 2
> a) *invent* (verb) means 'to think of ideas for things that no-one
>   has ever made before, and then make them'
> b) *invention* (noun) is something which someone has invented
> 3
> a) *grandfather* is in the second sentence and option C
>   *competition* is in the first sentence and option A
>   *mother* is in the third sentence and option B
> b) she wanted to help someone else with a problem.
>   The correct option is B

✓ Exam task

Ask the students to read the whole text before answering the
questions. Encourage them to try to eliminate the incorrect
options in the same way they did in Exercise 4. Remind
students of the information in the second exam tip; tell them
that question 5 is about the whole text. Check answers.

> **Answers**   1 B   2 C   3 C   4 A   5 B

CLIL Science: Students work in groups. Each group thinks of
a common, everyday problem (e.g. I keep losing my phone,
or my headphones get tangled up in my pocket) and try to
come up with an invention which could solve that problem.
They should explain the materials they would use for their
invention. The problem and invention should then be
presented to the class, using pictures and oral explanation.

Travel

Reading & Writing Part 5

Grammar – Superlative adjectives

1 Encourage the students to talk about what they can see
in the photo and to answer the questions.

> **Sample answers**   It's a busy crossing in Asia.
> It's Shibuya crossing (in Japan).

2 Encourage the students to say what other information
they find out about the Shibuya crossing, e.g. *hundreds of
people cross the road every time the lights change, there's a
statue of a dog, many young people meet there.* You could
tell students the story of the dog, Hachikō, who waited
every day at Shibuya station for his master to come
back from work – sadly, his master died at work one day,
but the dog went back every day for nine years. Have a

brief class discussion on famous landmarks in students'
town(s), e.g. a town square, a shopping centre, a large
roundabout or a special building or statue.

3 Students underline the examples of the superlative
adjectives in Exercise 2 and say what the difference is
between comparative and superlative adjectives, e.g.
we use superlative adjectives to compare one thing
with many things (comparative adjectives compare
two things), we add the ... *-est* to short adjectives (with
comparatives, we add *-er* and *than*) and we usually add
the most to longer adjectives (*more* to comparative
adjectives). Refer students to the spelling rules for
superlative adjectives in the Grammar reference on page
97 before they do this. Check the students' spelling. Then
put students into teams and give them a few minutes to
memorise the information. With books closed, ask each
team a question, e.g. *What is the longest bridge in the
world? Where is it? How long is it?*

> **Answers**   2 The longest   3 The biggest   4 the oldest
> 5 the worst

CLIL Geography (Web page): In small groups, the students
look for information about superlative places, buildings,
transport, etc. in the world, e.g. the widest bridge, the
biggest park. The students then write content for a web
page for the other groups. When the groups have found
the answers, they make a poster to illustrate some of the
superlative things they have found.

4 Remind the students that in Reading & Writing Part 5,
they have to complete each gap in a text with one word.
Read the exam tip as a class. Remind the students to read
the complete sentence before they start writing.

> **Answers**   1 most   2 than   3 are   4 not   5 to   6 were

✓ Exam task

Students read the complete email first. Ask some general
questions, e.g. *Where is Zeynep? How did she get there?
What's the place like?*, before they start writing.

> **Answers**   1 are   2 by   3 to   4 most   5 ago   6 than

▶ *See the Workbook and online resources for further practice.*

Speaking Part 2 (Phase 1)

1 Ask students to tell you what they remember about
Speaking Part 2 Phase 1 first. If necessary, they can look
back at the exam task in Unit 3 on page 22 to remind
themselves what they have to do.

Ask students not to look at Exercise 2 yet. In pairs, they
suggest some adjectives to complete the questions in
Exercise 1. Don't check answers yet.

2 🔊 **21** Listen to check answers to the first question in Exercise 1. Then, students complete Leyla's answers. If necessary, play the recording twice.

Answers	Not; ill

Recording script

Examiner:	Do you think going to school by boat is <u>exciting</u>, Leyla?
Leyla:	<u>Not</u> really.
Examiner:	Why not?
Leyla:	Because I sometimes feel <u>ill</u> on boats.

3 🔊 **22** Ask students to listen for the answer to the second question in Exercise 1. Then check answers.

Answer	Why?

Recording script

Examiner:	Do you think going to school by train is <u>fun</u>, Tomas?
Tomas:	No. Trains are crowded in my city, and you often have to stand up.
Examiner:	What do you think, Leyla?
Leyla:	I like travelling by train.
Examiner:	<u>Why</u>?
Leyla:	Because it's fast.

4 🔊 **22** Go over the exam tip together. Then, play the recording again. Students compare answers in pairs. Check answers. If necessary, play the recording a third time to check answers.

Answers	1 Because the trains are crowded in his city, and you often have to stand up.
	2 Because it's fast.

5 Remind the students that they should try to use different words and expressions to their partner in this part of the exam. Point out that it is important to show the examiner the language they know. They should not just repeat what their partner says. Students do the exercise in pairs.

Sample answers	2 there is so much traffic
3 you travel for free	

6 🔊 **23** Encourage the students to suggest possible ways to complete the question. Play the recording to check their answers.

Answer	like best

Recording script

Examiner:	So, Leyla, which of these ways of travelling to school do you <u>like best</u>?

☑ Exam task

Remind the students to give reasons for their answers. You could ask two or three pairs to answer the questions in front of the class. The rest of the class listens and decides who gives the best reason for each question.

UNIT OBJECTIVES

A2 KEY FOR SCHOOLS TOPICS: education, entertainment

GRAMMAR: *must / mustn't, should / shouldn't, can/could*, adverbs of manner

VOCABULARY: education, musical instruments

READING & WRITING PART 1: looking for words with a similar meaning; **PART 6:** checking spelling before finishing

LISTENING PART 2: choosing the correct answer

SPEAKING PART 1: answering questions about school and study

Education

Grammar & Vocabulary

STARTER
Focus students' attention on the title of this unit and the picture. Encourage them to say what the unit is about, i.e. schools, school subjects. Brainstorm names of school subjects and write a list on the board. Try to elicit all the subjects used as answers in Exercise 1. Students will talk about the subjects they study at school in the Speaking section of this unit.

1 Go over the example with the class. Students do the exercise in pairs.

> **Answers** 2 art 3 music 4 history 5 English 6 science
> 7 geography

2 After checking answers as a class, students work in pairs taking turns to ask and answer the questions.

> **Answers** 1 teach 2 miss 3 take 4 learn 5 spend

Grammar – *must / mustn't*

3 If necessary, pre-teach 'school rule' by giving some examples, e.g. *Do you have to wear a school uniform? Can you eat in class?* Students underline the words, then say what word we use to talk about rules and obligation *(must)*. Focus on the form by asking questions, e.g. *What is the negative form of 'must'? (mustn't) Is 'must' followed by the -ing form or the infinitive? (infinitive without to) Do we use 'must' for all persons, I, you, he, etc.? (Yes)*

> **Answers**
> 1 No, she can't. (We <u>must wear jackets</u> and tights all year, even in the <u>summer</u>.)
> 2 No, they can't. (You <u>mustn't</u> walk or <u>sit on the grass in winter</u>)

4 Encourage the students to read the complete sentences first before they start writing. Refer students to the Grammar reference on page 98.

> **Answers** 2 mustn't use 3 mustn't take 4 must wear
> 5 must walk

FURTHER PRACTICE
With students at the same school, students write some school rules for a perfect school. If they go to different schools, they write their real school rules and then find out who goes to the strictest school.

Grammar – *should / shouldn't*

5 Ask the students to underline the words in the conversation which say it's a good idea *(should)* and it isn't a good idea *(shouldn't)* to do something. Highlight the form of *should* either by referring the students to the Grammar reference on page 99 or by asking questions, e.g. *What's the negative form of should? (shouldn't) What form of the verb follows 'should'? (the infinitive without to) Do we use the same form of 'should' for all persons?* (Yes). After checking the answers, invite a brief classroom discussion on whether the students agree with the boy.

> **Answers** 1 Yes 2 No

6 This exam advice has been taken from the Examiner's Report for the *A2 Key for Schools* exams (see www.cambridgeenglish.org).

> **Answers**
> 2 shouldn't worry; should be
> 3 should answer
> 4 should check
> 5 shouldn't write; should use

▶ *See the Workbook and online resources for further practice.*

Reading & Writing Part 1

1 Encourage the students to look at the exam task and to say what they have to do. If necessary, remind them that in Reading & Writing Part 1, they have to read a notice or message and decide which option (A, B or C) means the same as the notice or message. The focus is on overall understanding. Point out that the students need to look for words which have a similar meaning in the notices, rather than the same words. Make sure they underline the important words only and not every word.

> **Answers**
> 2 You should <u>bring</u> your <u>teacher</u> a <u>note</u> if you <u>miss a class</u>. b (should write to the school)
> 3 You said she wants it on Friday, but actually <u>she wants it tomorrow</u>! a (must take her homework to school tomorrow)
> 4 <u>No running inside</u> the school building. a (must walk at all times in the school)

2 Do this pre-exam task exercise together as a class. Point out that it is important to read and understand the whole text and avoid just looking for synonyms.

> **Answers**
> In A, *give back* means the same as *return*.
> In C, *put back* means the same as *return*. Option C also contains *right*, which means the same as *correct*.

✓ Exam task

Encourage the students to try to identify the overall meaning of the message or notice first. Then, they should look for words in options A, B or C which have a similar meaning to words in the message or notice.

> **Answers**   1 C   2 B   3 A   4 A   5 B   6 C

When you have checked students' answers, ask students to work in small groups and write a list of notices in their school(s), e.g. *Boys' and Girls' Changing Rooms, No running, Turn off all mobile phones, Be quiet, English class, Speak English!*

Entertainment

Grammar & Vocabulary

1 Encourage the students to think of some more musical instruments.

> **Sample answers**
> I can see a piano, a drum, a keyboard and what's this? I think it's a violin. (Other instruments include: guitar, clarinet, recorder, saxophone, xylophone, trumpet, cello.)

2 Ask the students to look at the picture first and to try to predict the answer before they read the text.

> **Answer**   She teaches music in her town's music school.

Grammar – *can/could*

3 Point out that the students should underline the answers in the text. Encourage the students to say which word we use to talk about ability in the present (*can / can't* + infinitive) and which word we use to talk about ability in the past (*could / couldn't* + infinitive). If necessary, refer the students to the table in the Grammar reference on page 99.

> **Answers**
> 1 Yes, before she was eleven. (When Camila was 11, <u>she could play the violin well</u>)
> 2 Because they don't have enough money to buy them. (<u>Most of her students can't buy</u> their own instruments because <u>they don't have enough money</u>)

4 Encourage the students to read the complete email before they start writing.

> **Answers**   2 can't sing   3 can learn   4 could sing
> 5 couldn't play   6 can write   7 can sing

5 Remind the students they need to use questions and answers with *can* and *could*. Brainstorm some questions and write them on the board first.

> **Sample questions and answers**
> Can you play an instrument? Yes, I can. I can play the violin.
> When did you start learning the violin? I could play it when I was seven.
> Can anyone in your family play an instrument? Yes, my brother can play the piano and my mum can play the violin like me.

▶ *See the Workbook and online resources for further practice.*

Listening Part 2

Grammar – Adverbs of manner

1 Students can discuss who they think it is in pairs.

Alternatively, with books closed, read the text sentence by sentence and students try to guess the famous person.

> **Answer**   It's Leonardo Da Vinci.

2 If necessary, point out that we use adverbs to describe how we do things (the verb). Ask students to say how we form adverbs in English (usually the adjective + *ly*) and point out that there are some irregular adverbs e.g. *good – well*.

> **Answers**   1 badly   2 well   3 beautifully

3 Students look at the spelling rules for adverbs in the Grammar reference on page 100 before they do this exercise.

> **Answers**   2 wonderful = wonderfully   3 easy = easily
> 4 good = well   5 bad = badly

CLIL Art: In small groups, the students use the internet to find some information about a famous artist. Then they prepare a short presentation for the class using PowerPoint. They should use *can/could* and adverbs in their presentation.

4 🔊 **24** Ask the students to look at the exam task and to say what they have to do in this part (complete some notes with a word, number, date or time). Read the exam tip together as a class, pointing out that although they may hear two possible answers, only one is correct. Play each recording twice. With a stronger class, encourage the students to say what the incorrect answer refers to (1a bring your instrument on Thursday; 2b I really enjoy history but ...; 3b a very important visitor is coming; 4a price in the bookshop; 5a we went there last year).

| Answers | 1 b | 2 a | 3 a | 4 b | 5 b |

Recording script

1

So, bring your instruments on Thursday for the final practice before the school concert. Remember (1) the concert is next Monday.

2ken

I really enjoy my history class because the teacher is very good but (2) I think I like geography best because I like learning about different countries and people from those places.

3

Listen carefully please. (3) Today your maths class will be one hour earlier at a quarter past eleven because later at twelve fifteen, we've got a very important visitor from the music school.

4

You all need to buy this book for your English class. The price is £4.99 in the bookshop but we are selling it here (4) in the school for the cheaper price of £3.50.

5

This year (5) we're going to the zoo with our science teacher. I don't know why we can't go to the water park again. We had a great time there last year.

✓ Exam task

🔊 **25** Ask the students to read the exam task and say what the recording is about. (A teacher is giving a new class some information.) Encourage the students to say what type of information is missing in each gap. (1 a time; 2 a phone number; 3 a school subject; 4 a type of shoe). Play the recording at least twice. Unlike the exam, this task has four not five items.

| Answers | 1 9.15 | 2 7885421 | 3 maths | 4 trainers | 5 £9.75 |

Recording script

You will hear a teacher talking to her new class.

Welcome to your first day at the Leonardo Da Vinci School of Art and Drama. (0) I'm Maria Muzzio – your teacher this year. However, despite my name, I am not Italian. I am actually British.

Please listen carefully to this information. You must all be in your classroom at nine o'clock every morning. I'll check your names and then (1) the first class begins at quarter past nine.

If you can't come to school because you're ill, for example, your parents should call me as soon as they can (2) on seven-double eight-five-four-two-one. When you come back to school you'll have to do any work you missed.

In the mornings, you'll all be together for (3) English, maths and science. In the afternoon, students on the Art programme will do art and music, while those on the Theatre programme have dance and drama.

(4) For afternoon classes, make sure you wear trainers. You can't dance in boots, or paint in sandals!

And finally, we have school sweaters for sale. The normal price is twelve pounds fifty but (5) they're only nine pounds seventy-five for first year students.

Any questions?

FURTHER PRACTICE

Write on the board: *1 Is the Leonardo Da Vinci School of Art and Drama different to your school? How? 2 Would you like to study there? Why (not)? 3 What would you like to study there? 4 What would you not like to study?* In pairs, students take turns to ask and answer these questions.

Speaking Part 1 (Phase 1 and 2)

1 Invite a brief class discussion on whether any of the students have been to an International Summer School, perhaps to study English. Then ask them to work in pairs to think of questions they would ask in a similar situation. Tell them to write down their questions.

> **Sample answers** Where do you live?
> What school do you go to?   What's your school like?
> What subjects do you study?   Do you study English?

2 🔊 **26** Play the recording twice. The first time, the students put a tick next to the questions they hear from Exercise 1. On the second listening, stop the recording after each question so the students have time to write it down.

> **Answers**
> 1 What's your name?
> 2 Where do you come from?
> 3 Do you study English at school?
> 4 What subjects do you study?
> 5 Which subjects do you like best?

Recording script

Wayne:	Hi, I'm Wayne. (1) What's your name?
Flor:	Hi, I'm Flor. It's a Spanish name. I'm from Argentina. (2) Where do you come from?
Wayne:	I'm from Capetown in South Africa. You can speak English really well. (3) Do you study English at school?
Flor:	Yes, we have English on Tuesdays and Thursdays. We also do our history lessons in English. (4) What subjects do you study?
Wayne:	Oh, the usual subjects like maths, English, science ... We also study French. (5) Which subjects do you like best?
Flor:	I love art and music. That's why I'm here at this summer school. What about you?
Wayne:	I love maths and computers so I'm going to do the computer course.
Flor:	Really? I don't like computers very much and I'm terrible at maths.

3 Point out that in Speaking Part 1, the examiner will ask each candidate very similar questions to these.

4 🔊 ㉗ Point out that Olga and Jorge are not asked exactly the same questions.

Answers

	Olga	Jorge	Both
1			✓
2		✓	
3	✓		
4			✓

Recording script

Examiner:	(1) Olga, do you study English at school?
Olga:	Yes, I do. We have English on Mondays, Wednesdays and Fridays.
Examiner:	(3) Which subjects do you like best?
Olga:	I like art and music.
Examiner:	Why?
Olga:	Because I'm good at drawing. I like music because I can play the piano well.
Examiner:	(4) What do you like about your school?
Olga:	I've got a lot of friends there and the teachers are very friendly.
Examiner:	Thank you. (1) Do you study English at school, Jorge?
Jorge:	Yes, and I also go to a language school in the afternoon.
Examiner:	(2) What other subjects do you study?
Jorge:	I study maths, art, music, history and science.
Examiner:	(4) What do you like about your school?
Jorge:	My friends.
Examiner:	Why?
Jorge:	Because we have a lot of fun together.

5 🔊 ㉗ Ask the students to say why Olga and Jorge give good answers (because they answer in complete sentences and not just one or two words). Read the exam tip together as a class. Point out that the missing words are all verbs.

Answers   Olga: 2 like   3 can play   4 've got
Jorge: 5 study   6 have

☑ Exam task

Remind the students to answer in full sentences and to take turns to be the examiner and the students.

Reading & Writing Part 6

1 Encourage the students to say what they can see in the picture first and what they think the boy is writing in his email.

2 Ask the students to underline Malik's three questions in his email first.

3 Read the exam tip as a class first. Point out that these are some of the most common spelling mistakes that A2 Key exam candidates make.

4 Also ask the students how many words they need to write in Writing Part 6 (25 words or more).

☑ Exam task

Brainstorm some possible answers to the questions before the students start writing.

5 Remind the students that they should always leave time to check their work before they finish.

We had a great time!

UNIT OBJECTIVES

A2 KEY FOR SCHOOLS TOPICS: holidays, personal experiences

GRAMMAR: past continuous, past simple & past continuous

VOCABULARY: holiday activities, adjectives of opinion

READING & WRITING PART 4: choosing A, B or C correctly; **PART 7:** using *because*, *so* and *while* to improve writing

LISTENING PART 5: listening for synonyms

SPEAKING PART 2: talking about likes and preferences

Holidays

Grammar & Vocabulary

STARTER
With books closed, ask students what they like doing on holiday. Elicit activities (e.g. going to restaurants, visiting cities) and places (e.g. going to a campsite, going to a new country).

1 Students take turns to ask and answer the questions in the quiz. Demonstrate this with a strong student, e.g.

Teacher: *When you're on holiday, do you prefer to A visit new countries? B visit your own country? or C stay at home?*

Student: *I prefer to visit new countries.*

2 Students can find the quiz results at the back of the Student's Book on page 133. Ask the students if they agree with the results.

3 Encourage the students to read the complete sentences first before they start writing.

> **Answers**   2 speak   3 try   4 have   5 learn   6 stay   7 visit

Grammar – Past continuous

4 Encourage the students to look at the picture and to tell you what the people are doing before they read the text.

> **Answers**   1 B   2 C   3 A

5 Ask the students if the activities in the text are happening now (present), later (future) or before (in the past). Check that the students can identify the past continuous. Encourage the students to say how we form the past continuous positive, negative, question and short answer. Point out that the spelling rules of the *-ing* form are the same as for the present continuous. If necessary, refer the students to the Grammar reference on page 100.

> **Answers**
> Students should underline: *it wasn't raining*, Dad *was building* a fire, my sister *was reading*, Kevin and I *were climbing* a tree.
> 1 Yesterday at 7 p.m.   2 No   3 No

6 With a stronger class, read the email to the class but stop before each verb to see if the students can provide the answer, e.g. *At 11 o'clock, the sun* [pause]

> **Answers**   1 was   2 wasn't   3 were   4 was   5 were
> 6 were

FURTHER PRACTICE
The students write a reply to Sandra's email answering the question *What were you doing at 11 o'clock yesterday?*

▶ *See the Workbook and online resources for further practice.*

Listening Part 5

1 Encourage students to tell you what they can remember about Listening Part 5 – they can look at the exam task to help. Point out that in the exam task, they have to match the places where the friends stayed with the friends. Refer students to the example in the exam task, where C (campsite) has already been matched with Liam.

> **Answers**
> 1 Victoria's talking to her dad about her friends and where they stayed on holiday.
> 2 Liam   3 at a campsite

2 Remind the students that they may not hear the same word in the recording; it may be another word or phrase with a similar meaning (this is called a synonym).

> **Answers**   1 B   2 E   3 A   4 C   5 D

3 🔊 **28** Point out that although the students will hear the words A–E on the recording, they should write one of the words 1–5 next to each name.

> **Answers**   1 2 clothes (a sweater)   2 3 a book (a dictionary)
> 3 5 a mobile (a phone)

Recording script

Sister:	What are you doing, Samuel?
Samuel:	I'm reading a message from Conor.
Sister:	Conor? Where is he?
Samuel:	He isn't having a good time on holiday. He says the music in the disco is terrible and (1) he forgot to pack his sweater and it's really cold at night.
Sister:	Oh, no! Can't he borrow one from his brother?
Samuel:	From Mark? He's in Italy learning Italian. And (2) Mark forgot to take his Italian dictionary so he had to buy a new one and it cost €20!
Sister:	Really! What a family!
Samuel:	That's nothing. Did you hear about Hanna? She's also in Italy.
Sister:	No, what did she do?
Samuel:	(3) She left her phone at home. When she got to the airport, the Italian family wasn't waiting for her. She didn't have their phone number because her address book is on the phone.
Sister:	What did she do?
Samuel:	Well, she found the information desk and they phoned her mum and her mum ...

✓ Exam task

🔊 **29** Look at the exam task as a class. Remind the students that they will hear the friends 0–5 in order. Encourage them to think of the words they might hear for each of the places A–H before they listen, e.g. A flat; B water, sea, lake; C tent, countryside; D castle; E country, animals; F home, family; G small hotel; H accommodation. Play the recording twice.

| **Answers** | 1 A   2 H   3 D   4 F   5 G |

Recording script

You will hear Victoria and her dad talking about places to stay on holiday. Where did each of her friends stay?

Dad:	Victoria, I've got a week's holiday soon. Why don't we go to the countryside and take the tent?
Victoria:	No! (0) My friend Liam slept in a tent last July and it rained all week.
Dad:	But I like the rain.
Victoria:	Dad! (1) Daniel went to Edinburgh last year. They rented a flat in the city centre. He said the castle's amazing.
Dad:	No, not a city! Where did Melissa and her parents go?
Victoria:	(2) They stayed in a small family hotel in a village in France. She said it was just like home.
Dad:	Mm. And did Alba go away?
Victoria:	Yeah. (3) She and her family stayed in a castle on Malta. They drove to Italy and took a boat from there.
Dad:	That's a lot of driving! Didn't your friend Martin go to Thailand?
Victoria:	Yes, with his dad. They were looking for a hotel when (4) a friend of theirs invited them to stay in his house.
Dad:	Well, we can't go to Thailand just for a week!
Victoria:	I know! (5) Olivia's family stayed near Stanton's Farm in a guest-house. We could take our bikes there.
Dad:	Now that's a good idea.

4 With a weaker class, make the questions together and write them on the board first.

> **Sample answers**
> How often do you visit capital cities? A lot! I love visiting capital cities. My favourite city is Paris.
> Do you like learning the language? No, not really. My parents often speak English.
> Do you like staying in a comfortable hotel? Of course, I do!
> Do you often try new dishes? Yes, I do. I love trying new food.
> Do you like having a rest? No, I prefer doing activities.
> Do you like exploring somewhere new? Yes, I do. I like seeing new places and finding out about them.

Reading & Writing Part 4

1 Encourage students to tell you what they remember about Reading & Writing Part 4 – they can look at the exam task to help. Then read the exam tip together. Ask students to discuss the options as they do the task. Remind them that some verbs can be used with more than one pair of answers.

| **Answers** | 1 f   2 c   3 e   4 a; b; c; f   5 a; d   6 a; d |

2 Before doing the task, write *gift, prize* and *present* on the board and ask students to make a sentence with each of them, e.g. *I want to buy a gift for my mum. I won a prize in the swimming competition. My friend gave me a present for my birthday.* Then ask students to do the task.

| **Answer** | B prize |

✓ Exam task

Encourage students to read the complete text to get a general idea before they start answering the questions. When they have finished, encourage the students to compare their answers in pairs and to say why the other two answers are incorrect.

| **Answers** | 1 B   2 C   3 A   4 A   5 B   6 C |

> **FURTHER PRACTICE**
> In small groups, the students ask and answer questions about an amazing holiday. This can be a real holiday or a dream holiday. If necessary, help the students with the questions, e.g. *Where did you go? When did you go? Where did you stay? What did you do there?*

Personal experiences

Grammar & Vocabulary

1 After completing the exercise, ask students to underline the adjectives in each of the sentences.

| **Answers** | 1 ✓   2 ✗   3 ✓   4 ✗   5 ✓   6 ✗   7 ✓ |

2 Encourage students to think about sentences they could use these adjectives in and complete the exercise. Students can then write new sentences for some of these adjectives in pairs, e.g. *We had a great time at the party. It was brilliant.*

> **Answers** Good: amazing, brilliant, excellent, exciting, funny, interesting, wonderful,
> Bad: boring, terrible, tiring

3 If appropriate, highlight the difference between adjectives ending in *-ed* and *-ing*, e.g. *I was very excit**ed*** (someone feels: adjective + *-ed*) because my holiday was *excit**ing*** (something is: adjective + *-ing*). Also point out that if we enjoy something, it is *fun* but something that makes you laugh is *funny*.

> **Answers** 2 funny = fun 3 bored = boring
> 4 exciting = excited 5 wonderfull = wonderful
> 6 confortable = comfortable

FURTHER PRACTICE

Write these questions on the board: *What was your last birthday like? What was your last school trip like? What was your last exam like? What was the last film you saw like?*

In pairs, the students take turns to ask these questions and answer them using the adjectives of opinion.

Grammar – Past simple & past continuous

4 Check that the students can identify the past simple and past continuous first. Elicit the rules for when we use the past simple and past continuous from the class by asking these questions: *Do we use the past simple or continuous when we describe activities happening at a moment and we're not interested when the activity started or finished?* (past continuous) *Do we use the past simple or continuous to talk about complete actions?* (past simple) *When do we use the past simple and continuous together?* (When we want to say an action happened in the middle of an activity) With a weaker class, it may be necessary to guide the students to these answers using the question, e.g. *In the first sentence, do we know when I started my homework?* (No) *Are we interested?* (No) *Did the phone interrupt my homework?* (Yes) *In the second sentence, did I check the tickets?* (Yes, it's a completed action). *What activity was happening when I checked the tickets?* (He was driving).

> **Answers** Underline: rang, checked
> Circle: was doing, was driving

5 Make sure that the students spell the past simple and the *-ing* form correctly. If necessary, refer them to the spelling rules in the Grammar reference on page 101. Then ask the students to underline the examples of *when* and circle the examples of *while*. Ask them to

say whether we usually use the past simple or past continuous after *while* (past continuous).

> **Answers** 1 swam 2 started 3 was packing
> 4 was studying 5 tried 6 were visiting

6 Point out that the students need to complete the questions in the past simple or past continuous. Then, in pairs, the students take turns to ask and answer the questions.

> **Sample answers**
> 1 Was it raining when you woke up this morning? No, it wasn't. The sun was shining.
> 2 What were you doing when the teacher came in? I was talking to my friends.
> 3 What did you watch on TV while you were having dinner yesterday? I didn't watch TV while I was having dinner.
> 4 Was your mum reading a book when you got home? No, she wasn't. She was reading a newspaper.

▶ *See the Workbook and online resources for further practice.*

Reading & Writing Part 7

1 Read the exam tip as a class and check that students understand the difference in meaning between the words (*because* tells us 'why', *so* tells us the result of an action and *while* tells us 'during the time that'). Encourage the students to compare their answers.

> **Answers** 1 so 2 while 3 because 4 because 5 while
> 6 so

2 Ask students to look at the picture and tell you what they think is happening. Try to elicit some vocabulary from the story and if necessary ask students some questions, e.g. *Where are they?* (At the airport) *What are they doing?* (They're having a coffee) *What is happening?* (They're late / They nearly missed the flight). Then ask students to do the task in pairs.

> **Answers** 1 while 2 so 3 Because

3 Remind students to use present tenses in this exercise. Ask them to complete the sentences and then compare their answers in groups.

> **Sample answers**
> 1 while he runs (for his flight). 2 so he is sleeping.
> 3 because her mother is taking a long time to check the bill.

4 Tell students to use past tenses to talk about the pictures in pairs or groups of three.

> **Sample answers**
> Picture 1 – They were at the beach. Some boys and girls were playing volleyball while / as a girl was walking along the beach.
> Picture 2 – She felt upset because the ball hit her. The other teenagers were worried.
> Picture 3 – The boy felt sorry, so he bought the girl an ice cream.

✓ Exam task

Remind students that they can use present or past tenses to tell the story, but point out that they will get higher marks for using past tenses. Remind them to use **because, while, so, and, when** and **as** if possible. Ask two or three students to read their stories to the class. Remind students that there is no single correct answer in Reading & Writing Part 7.

> **Sample answer**
> Some boys and girls were playing volleyball. A girl was looking at her phone while she walked along the beach. Suddenly, the volleyball hit the girl on the head. She felt upset and the boys and girls were worried because they thought she was hurt. One of the boys bought the girl an ice cream and she felt much happier.

Speaking Part 2 (Phase 2)

1 Before Speaking Part 2 Phase 2 begins, the examiner will take away the pictures that are used in Phase 1. In this exercise, pictures are used to introduce the topic before students focus on talking about preferences, which they might have to do in Phase 2.

Ask students what they can see in the pictures. Elicit some vocabulary related to the pictures, e.g. *pool, camping, sightseeing*. Students work in pairs do the task.

> **Answers**   A is the third picture   B is the second picture
> C is the first picture

2 Read the exam tip together and tell students that they are going to read a conversation between an examiner and two candidates. Check that students remember the difference between *like* and *would like*. If necessary, refer them to the Speaking bank on page 63. Students fill in the gaps in pairs.

> **Answers**   1 like   2 would like / 'd like   3 like
> 4 would like / 'd like

3 🔊 **30** Before playing the recording, remind students that *would like* is usually contracted to *'d like* in spoken English, so they need to listen carefully to hear the difference in pronunciation between *like* and *'d like*. Students check their answers in pairs.

> **Recording script**
> Examiner: What activities would you like to do on your next holiday, Cari?
> Cari: Well, I like the beach, and on my next holiday I'd like to learn to surf.
> Examiner: Why?
> Cari: Because I've seen people surfing on TV, and it looks fun.
> Examiner: What about you, Mehmet? What activities would you like to do on your next holiday?
> Mehmet: I like going to the mountains, and I'd like to go skiing again. It's so exciting!

4 In pairs, one student asks the first question from the conversation and the other student answers. Then students change roles.

5 🔊 **31** Read the exam tip as a class. Remind students that in Speaking Part 2 Phase 2, the examiner asks each candidate the same two questions. The candidates have to answer and say why. Read the exam task and then play the recording. Students do the task. Play the recording again if necessary.

> **Recording script**
> Examiner: Cari, when you go on holiday, do you prefer camping, or staying in a hotel?
> Cari: Well, camping is OK, but I don't like insects very much, and I like to be comfortable, so I prefer a hotel really.

> **Answers**   Cari prefers staying in a hotel.
> Her reasons are that she doesn't like insects, and she likes to be comfortable.

✓ Exam task

Go over the instructions with the students. Remind students to answer in full sentences and to answer the question 'Why?'.

> **Sample answers**
> I prefer to go camping **because** I really enjoy spending time outdoors and playing outdoors games.
> I think it's better to go on holiday with a few people **because** if you go with a big group, you are always waiting for everybody to get ready and that can take a long time.

CLIL Geography: In pairs or small groups, students choose a dream holiday destination. They research the destination and produce an advertisement giving details about the destination (they can look at information about real destinations on the internet for inspiration). Following this, each group can look at each other's advertisements and choose their favourite destination. They should ask questions to help them make their decision (e.g. *When is it hot there? How much does it cost?*).

UNIT OBJECTIVES

A2 KEY FOR SCHOOLS TOPICS: entertainment & media, television

GRAMMAR: *be going to*, infinitives & *-ing* forms

VOCABULARY: entertainment, television, word-building

READING & WRITING PART 3: recognising opinions, likes and preferences; **PART 6:** using *and*, *or*, *but* and *because* to improve writing

LISTENING PART 4: answering questions about the past, the present and the future

SPEAKING PART 1: answering questions about future plans

Entertainment & media

Reading & Writing Part 3

STARTER
With books closed, brainstorm a list of types of entertainment, e.g. concert, circus, film, play. Invite a brief class discussion on what people can see in the students' town and where they can find information about what's on.

1 Point out that this is a programme from an arts centre.

> **Answers**   2 film   3 dance   4 circus   5 exhibition

FURTHER PRACTICE
In pairs, students talk about the things they'd like to see, e.g. *Would you like to see the film? No thanks! I don't like adventure films. Would you like to see the dance competition? Yes, because I love dancing.*

2 Read the exam tip together. Remind students that the text may use different words to the questions. Students do the task in pairs. Check answers as a class.

> **Answers**
> 1 She thinks it was good. (I usually enjoy his films, and this was no different.)
> 2 She didn't like the ending. (It's a pity the filmmakers decided to change the ending.)

3 Point out that it is usually a good idea for students to read the questions before they read the text so that they are reading for a specific purpose. After students read question 1 and the first paragraph in the exam task, work through the questions as a class to show students how to eliminate the incorrect multiple-choice options and choose the correct answer.

> **Answers**
> 1 No, she doesn't say that she chose this, and she doesn't say that she likes it.
> 2 She says 'there's no timetable. I can do my classes at any time.' She says 'That's the best thing.' so she likes it.
> 3 Yes. She says 'I have to do all the same subjects as other students.' but the text doesn't say if she chooses them.
> 4 B

✓ Exam task

Remind students to complete the exam task using the approach suggested in the previous exercise. (First read the question, then try to eliminate all the incorrect options before selecting the correct one.) When checking answers, ask students to explain why the other answers are incorrect using information from the text where possible. Remind students that in the exam, question 5 can be a more general question about the whole text.

> **Answers**   2 A   3 C   4 B   5 C

Grammar – *be going to*: positive & negative

4 Students work in pairs to answer the questions. Check answers as a class.

> **Answers**
> 1 I'm not going to see my family for a few weeks.
> 2 … people from a real circus are going to teach us what they do in their shows.
> 3 because she's talking about things planned for the future.

5 Refer the students to the Grammar reference on page 101 and highlight the form of *be going to*: positive and negative before they do this exercise. Encourage the students to read the text first and answer the question *What is Madison going to do in the summer holidays?* before writing.

> **Answers**
> 2 isn't / 's not going to meet
> 3 is / 's going to dance
> 4 are / 're going to spend   5 are / 're going to do
> 6 are / 're going to have   7 isn't / 's not going to be
> 8 am / 'm not going to see   9 are going to watch

▶ *See the Workbook and online resources for further practice.*

1 Accept any appropriate suggestions from the students.

2 🔊 32 Tell students to just listen for the answers without writing anything the first time they listen. Play the recording. Then play the recording again. Students write and compare their answers in pairs. Less able students could be told that all the answers are places.

> **Answers** 1 in the park 2 at the stadium
> 3 in the sports centre

> **Recording script**
>
> Fabio: Have you heard about the free rock concert next weekend?
> Reyha: No. (1) <u>Is it going to be in the park?</u>
> Fabio: It was last year, but it rained, so this year (2) <u>they're playing at the stadium</u>, as it's got a roof.
> Reyha: Well, I'll definitely go. (3) <u>The only concert I've ever been to was in the sports centre</u>, so it wasn't very big.

3 🔊 32 Play the recording a third time for students to check their answers to Exercise 2 and answer the question in Exercise 3. Check answers as a class.

> **Answer** At the stadium

4 Read the exam tip together. Highlight that it is important for students to consider whether questions in the exam refer to the past, the present or the future.

> **Answers** 1 future 2 present 3 past

5 Students read question 1 in the exam task and answer the questions in pairs. Explain that it is helpful for them to think about other words which might connect to the answers before they listen.

> **Answers** A film A museum or gallery

✓ Exam task

🔊 33 Give students time to read the questions before they listen. Remind them to think of other words which they might hear for each answer option. Students listen to the recording twice. Check answers as a class.

> **Answers**
> 1 C 2 B 3 C 4 A 5 B

> **Recording scripts**
>
> 1 *You will hear two friends talking about their plans for the weekend. What do they decide to do?*
> Girl 1: What shall we do this weekend? Are there any good films on?
> Girl 2: I'm going to the cinema this evening – I don't want to go twice. What about that photography exhibition you mentioned that you want to see?
> Girl 1: But you don't like photography. How about a concert?
> Girl 2: There's nothing on that I fancy seeing. It's OK. (1) <u>Let's go and see the photos.</u>
>
> 2 *You will hear a boy asking his friend Andres about yesterday evening. What was Andres doing?*
> Boy: What were you doing when I called you yesterday, Andres? It sounded fun!
> Andres: (2) <u>My sister was showing me a video that her friend has posted on a website.</u> It's of him playing a computer game.
> Boy: Oh, that actually sounds rather boring!
> Andres: Not at all! It's really fun! He's so good at it. He's going to be on TV soon.
>
> 3 *You will hear a girl leaving a message about a competition. What does the girl want to do in the competition?*
> Girl: Hi, Marco. I'm calling about the competition. I know you want us to dance together, but I think lots of people will dance, so I want to do something different. I'm fairly good at the piano now, and I've got a good song to play. It's one you know. (3) <u>Why don't you sing it and I'll accompany you?</u> Call me!
>
> 4 *You will hear two friends talking about going to a museum. How are they going to travel?*
> Girl: I looked online to see where the museum is. There's a train station pretty near it.
> Boy: (4) <u>Oh, I forgot to say – my brother's happy to drive us there. It's on his way to work.</u>
> Girl: Doesn't your brother go to work by bus?
> Boy: He's just passed his driving test, so no more buses for him!
> Girl: Or for us! That's great. Thanks.
>
> 5 *You will hear a boy talking about a concert. Why is he going to the concert?*
> Boy: I'm really sorry, but I can't go out with you tomorrow. I forgot that I'm going to a concert. The Kingpins are playing. (5) <u>I don't really like them but they're my sister's favourite – she's mad about them.</u> Why don't you come? There are still tickets for sale. And I know your friend Emin will be there. He's always singing Kingpins songs!

Television

Speaking Part 1 (Phase 2)

1 The TV programmes in this exercise are the ones that appear on the Key for Schools vocabulary list but brainstorm other types of TV programmes, e.g. reality show, talent show, documentary. This will help the students do Exercise 2.

> **Answers**   2 the weather   3 the news   4 quiz show

2 Encourage the students to answer in full sentences giving reasons with *because*. Then ask students to give a brief report to the class about their partner's favourite TV programmes.

> **Sample answers**   1 I watch TV every day after dinner.
> 2 I like watching sports programmes because I love all kinds of sports.
> 3 I don't like watching cartoons because they are boring and they are for children.

3 Read the exam tip as a class. Point out that all the questions in this exercise ask about future plans and highlight the question. If necessary, refer the students to the Grammar reference on page 102. Also point out that the first word in each question begins with a capital letter.

> **Answers**
> 2 What are you going to watch on TV later?
> 3 Are you going to see a film tomorrow?
> 4 What are you going to do at the weekend?
> 5 Are you going to do anything special on Saturday night?
> 6 What are your plans for next week?

4 Monitor as the students are asking and answering the questions. Make a note of any mistakes and go over these as a class when they have finished the activity. You could ask some pairs to ask and answer a question for the whole class.

5 🔊 34 Point out that the examiner doesn't ask Ella and Emir the same question.

> **Answers**   Ella: 4   Emir: 6

> **Recording script**
> Examiner: Now Ella, <u>what are you going to do at the weekend</u>?
> Ella: With friends.
> Examiner: Thank you. Emir, <u>what are your plans for next week</u>?
> Emir: I'm going to go to school of course. I'm also going to see a film at the cinema with my friends.

6 🔊 34 A stronger class might be able to answer this without listening again. Students should justify their answers.

> **Answers**   Emir because he answers the examiner's question in full sentences with *going to*.

✅ Exam task

Ask the students to take turns to be the examiner and candidate. Remind the candidate to answer in a complete sentence with the correct form of **be going to**.

> **Sample answers**
> What are you going to do this evening? After this class, I'm going to walk home. I'm going to do my homework and watch TV.
> What are your plans for the next school holidays? I think I'm going to stay at my grandparents' house.

Grammar & Vocabulary

Grammar – Infinitives & *-ing* forms

1 Encourage the students to look at the photo and to say what they can see. It is a photo of the WOMAD festival, which is an international arts festival. Ask the students if there is a WOMAD festival in their country.

Background information (see http://womad.org)

There are WOMADs in over 27 countries. There is a five-minute video on youtube introducing this festival (http://www.youtube.com/watch?v=5WpSafFS6PI).

> **Answer**
> The Kodō Drummers from Japan, the National Dance Company of Cambodia, a jazz band from India and the circus.

2 Refer the students to the Grammar reference on page 102 and ask the students to say when we use an infinitive (after some verbs and after an adjective) and an *-ing* form (after some verbs and after a preposition). Point out that students will have to learn which verbs are followed by an infinitive and which are followed by an *-ing* form. Encourage the students to underline the main verbs in the sentences (e.g. sentence 1 = *love*) and then elicit the correct form of the following verb.

> **Answers**
> 2 is to play = is playing
> 3 hope see = hope to see
> 4 I want invite you = I want to invite you
> 5 I need tell you = I need to tell you
> 6 I would love helping = I would love to help

3 Encourage the students to read the complete email first before they start writing.

> **Answers**   1 watching   2 listening   3 to see   4 to buy
> 5 to show   6 to hear

CLIL Music: Students work in small groups. Each group should look at the WOMAD website (http://womad.org) and choose a WOMAD festival in a particular country. They then find out whatever they can about that festival, including when it is, and what type of music there will be. They then give a presentation to the rest of the class (including music), who can ask questions and take notes.

Vocabulary – Word-building

4 Remind the students of the spelling rules, i.e. double the letter and add -er when it's a short rather than long vowel sound, e.g. *mm* in *drummer*; -r for words ending in -er e.g. *dancer*; add -er for words ending in other letters.

> **Answers** 2 writer 3 dancer 4 photographer 5 singer
> 6 painter

5 Remind the students to count the spaces as these tell them how many letters are missing.

> **Answers** 1 artist 2 musician 3 actor 4 secretary
> 5 journalist

FURTHER PRACTICE
Students talk together about the things they'd like to see at an Arts festival. They could write a message for a class blog, e.g. *I'd like to listen to cool music and see my favourite musicians. I hope to see something new and exciting, for example, I love watching dancers from other countries.*

CLIL Music: In small groups, students find some information about a type of music, e.g. jazz, classical, opera, folk, rap. Each group produces a short presentation with information about famous musicians, instruments, concerts and a short sound or video clip to illustrate their chosen type of music.

▶ *See the Workbook and online resources for further practice.*

Reading & Writing Part 6

1 Invite a brief class discussion on what the students have to do in this part. If necessary, ask the students to look at the exam task first. Read the exam tip as a class.

> **Answers** 1 b 2 c 3 d 4 e 5 a

2 First check that the students have understood what each connector means by asking them to say which word says why / gives a reason (*because*), which word adds more information (*and*), which word shows two or more possibilities (*or*) and which word introduces a contrast (*but*).

> **Answers**
> 2 We aren't going to the dance festival because there aren't any tickets left.
> 3 We can see a play and / or a film.
> 4 Don't forget to see the Drummers of Burundi and don't forget to bring your camera.
> 5 I don't like acting in plays but I like watching them.

3 Read the exam task as a class and ask the students to say who they need to write to (a friend) and how many pieces of information they need to include (three). Read the student's answer and point out that if the marker can't read a student's answer, he or she won't be able to give a mark.

> **Answer** The teacher asks Anatoly to rewrite his answer.

4 As a follow-up, the students say how many marks (out of five) they think Anatoly's answer will get. The students should justify their answer. Point out that Anatoly's answer is now a model answer and gets full marks; it starts and finishes well, it includes all three pieces of information and it is over 25 words.

> **Answers** 2 or 3 but

5 Brainstorm a list of possible shows as a class first. Remind students to use *and*, *but*, *because* and *or* in their answers.

> **Sample answer**
> Hi Sunita,
> I am going to see the Beijing circus next week in Central Park. Would you like to come with me? You'll love it because you love clowns.
> It starts at 3 p.m. but I think we should meet earlier. What about 2:30 outside the ticket office? You can get the number 13 bus there or you can cycle – it's not far.
> Speak soon,

6 Remind the students to leave time in the exam to check their work. Students can often learn a lot from reading each other's work. If appropriate, encourage the students to read each other's exam task and to use the writing checklist to say if it is a good answer.

Are you an outdoors person?

UNIT OBJECTIVES

A2 KEY FOR SCHOOLS TOPICS: the natural world, weather

GRAMMAR: *will / won't* and *may*, first conditional

VOCABULARY: places in the countryside, prepositions of place, weather

READING & WRITING PART 1: looking for words with a similar meaning (*not* + adjective); **PART 7:** checking spelling

LISTENING PART 1: deciding where things are

SPEAKING PART 2: describing activities, agreeing and disagreeing

The natural world

Listening Part 1

STARTER
Encourage the students to look at the map and identify the places A–H.

1 Students match the places A–H with the words 1–8. Check answers as a class.

> **Answers**   2 F   3 B   4 D   5 H   6 C   7 E   8 A

2 Point out that the students need to look at the map in Exercise 1 as they follow the instructions. Encourage the students to draw Ned's route with a pencil.

> **Answer**   Put a cross (✗) under the first picnic table (on the left).

3 Read the exam tip as a class and point out that the students will often hear prepositions of place, e.g. *behind, under, in, on*. Ask the students to read through Ned's instructions in Exercise 2 again and underline the prepositions of place (*through, across, through, behind, under, on the left*). Encourage the students to say where George's ball is using the preposition.

> **Answers**   A: It's next to a tree.   B: It's under the table.
> C: It's behind the gate.

4 🔊 **35** Play the recording twice so that the students can listen for the words. Ask the students to say what the other two pictures refer to. (The ball was under the table; Tom threw it behind the gate). Point out that students should try to eliminate the wrong answers in the exam in this way.

> **Answer**   Mum says: Look it's there, next to the tree.

Recording script
Where is George's ball?

George: Mum, I can't find the ball. Have you seen it?

Mum: It was under the table a minute ago.

George: Yes, and then Tom threw it behind that gate, but I've looked there.

Mum: Look it's there, next to the tree.

✓ Exam task

🔊 **36** Encourage the students to look at each set of pictures and to describe what they can see in each and if appropriate, say where things are. Point out that the students will hear each recording twice. Encourage the students to compare their answers in pairs and to say what the other two pictures refer to.

> **Answers**   1 B   2 C   3 B   4 A   5 C

Recording script
Look at question 1.

1 *Where will Joel and his family stay this year?*

Joel: Dad, can we go to that hotel next to the river again this year?

Dad: Sorry, Joel. Your mother didn't like it very much.

Joel: How about that place on top of that hill? We stayed there two years ago.

Dad: That's full, so (1) Mum and I found one in Great Woods. I booked it last night.

Now listen again.

2 *How much do Daniella's walking boots cost on the website?*

Daniella: I saw some great new walking boots in town today but they were £120.

Mum: Oh, Daniella, why don't you look online? Your cousin bought some boots for £100.

Daniella: (2) I looked at www.bestboots.com and the cheapest ones were £130.

Mum: Oh, really? Let's go and buy them from that shop in town then.

Now listen again.

3 *What time does the park close today?*

Girl: Excuse me. Do you know what time the park closes?

Man: The sign says it shuts at six thirty every day. (3) Oh, except Sunday, when it closes at six. That's today, isn't it?

Girl: Yes, that's right. What time is it now?

Man: Five thirty – so it's nearly time to go.

Now listen again.

4 What will they do in the afternoon?

Girl: That was awesome! I've never been windsurfing on this lake before.

Boy: I come here a lot. It's great, isn't it? Do you know what we're going to do next?

Girl: (4) <u>My dad said that after lunch we're going to build a tree house</u>.

Boy: Cool! And tomorrow we're going mountain biking. I love being outdoors in the school holidays!

Now listen again.

5 Where are Dad's keys?

Dad: I can't find my car keys. I thought I left them on that bag.

Girl: Look on the floor. Maybe you dropped them.

Dad: They're not here. (5) <u>I think they may still be inside the car.</u>

Girl: I'll look … <u>You're right, Dad, here they are!</u>

Now listen again.

Grammar – will / won't & may

5 Ask students if the sentences are referring to the present, past or future (Answer: future). Check students understand *certain, possible, impossible* before they do the exercise.

> **Answers**   1 b   2 c   3 a

6 Highlight the forms of *will* and *may*. Point out that the negative of *will* is *won't* and the question form is *Will you …?* Also point out that *will* and *may* are the same for all persons (*I, you, he* …) and after these words, we use the infinitive without *to*. If necessary, refer the students to the Grammar reference on page 103.

> **Answers**   2 am arrive = will arrive
> 3 will do you came = will you come
> 4 You maybe have = You may have

7 Encourage the students to read the complete conversation before they start writing. Ask fast finishers to continue the conversation using *will / won't* and *may*.

> **Answers**   2 may rain   3 will you get   4 may go
> 5 may drive   6 'll take / will take   7 won't be / will not be
> 8 'll have / will have

▶ *See the Workbook and online resources for further practice.*

Weather

Reading & Writing Part 1

1 With books closed, invite a brief discussion on the weather, e.g. *What's the weather like today? What was the weather like yesterday? What will the weather be like tomorrow?* After completing the exercise, ask students to make adjectives for the weather nouns (all except thunderstorm): *cloudy, foggy, icy, rainy, snowy, stormy, sunny, windy.*

> **Answers**   2 wind   3 rain   4 thunderstorm   5 fog   6 cloud

2 If necessary, point out that seasons are very different all over the world. This will depend on the hemisphere and also how close to the Equator the country is. Invite a brief class discussion on which of the places in this exercise the students would like to visit.

> **Answers**   2 winter   3 autumn   4 spring

FURTHER PRACTICE

In small groups, students discuss the question *When is the best time to visit your country?* They choose a reporter from the group who gives the rest of the class their group's opinion and reasons.

CLIL Geography/Maths: In small groups, students choose a city from a very different part of the world and write a short answer for the website question: *When is the best time to visit your city?* The students should find information about the city's weather and seasons and present this information using a weather map, a temperature bar chart and rainfall graph. Encourage the students to calculate the average rainfall and average temperatures per month, season and year. The group's answer should include a map to show where it is, a photo of the place and the information about the weather. As a class, read all the answers and vote on the best place to visit in winter, spring, summer and autumn. The Kids World Travel Guide website (http://www.kids-world-travel-guide.com) has travel information for young people, including information about the weather.

3 With books closed, encourage the students to close their eyes and imagine they're in a large park in the countryside. It's a beautiful summer's day. Ask the students to say what they can see (children playing, a lot of trees, grass, etc.). Then ask them to say if they can see any notices and elicit what is on them.

> **Sample answers**   Messages: Bring your football. Do we need a picnic blanket? Where exactly shall we meet?
> Notices: No cycling, Don't walk on the grass, Don't climb the trees, etc.

4 Encourage the students to look at the exam task and to say what they have to do in this part. (Read a notice, email or message and choose the correct answer from three options.)

5 Read the exam tip as a class first. Remind the students to look for *not* + opposites in this exercise.

> **Answers**   2 closed   3 running   4 over   5 dry   6 easy

✓ Exam task

Remind the students that they won't find exactly the same words in the notices and messages. They should look for words with a similar meaning. Also remind the students to cross out the answer as they find it.

FURTHER PRACTICE

Divide the class in half. In pairs, students in one half choose a new place, e.g. a museum, an airport, a sports centre, a town centre, a festival, and write three notices. Then in small groups, they take turns to read out their three notices. The other members of the group try to guess where they can see these notices, e.g.

A: *Our notices are No food or drink, No photography and Free entrance on Mondays 5–7 p.m.*

B: *Can you see them in a museum?*

Students in the other half of the class work in pairs to write a short email or text message. They should write an invitation, a cancellation or a change of plans message. Then they read their message to another pair who decide which of the three they have written, e.g.

A: *We wrote Dear Anna, I'm sorry but I can't come to the cinema tonight because my mum says I have to go to bed early. Sorry!*

B: *Is that a cancellation?*

Grammar – First conditional

6 Ask the students to look at the cartoon and to say what they can see first, e.g. countryside, field, gate, notice, cow, farmer.

> **Answers**   1 No, the gate is closed.   2 The cows are in the field.   3 No, the farmer isn't angry because he's asleep/sleeping.

7 Focus the students' attention on the two conditional sentences in Exercise 6 (*If the gate's open, the cows will run away; the farmer won't be pleased if the cows run away*) and highlight the form and use of the first conditional: *If* + present simple (possible situation), *will / won't* + infinitive (possible result) (or *will / won't* + infinitive *if* + present simple). If necessary, refer the students to the Grammar reference on page 104. Remind students that *will* and *won't* are always followed by the infinitive without *to*. Point out that we use a comma ',' in the girl's sentence *If the gate's open*, … because this sentence begins with *If*. The boy's sentence *The farmer won't be pleased* … begins with the result, so we don't use a comma ','. Encourage the students to read the complete conversation before they start writing. Ask fast finishers to continue the conversation using the first conditional.

> **Answers**   2 won't get / will not get   3 'll find / will find
> 4 'll we do / will we do   5 find   6 find
> 7 won't stay / will not stay   8 'll phone / will phone
> 9 get   10 doesn't answer / does not answer
> 11 'll call / will call

▶ *See the Workbook and online resources for further practice.*

1 Ask the students to look at the exam task and to say what they have to do in this part: look at three pictures and write a story. Ask students to read the whole text first and then try to correct the underlined words. Students check with a partner by spelling out the new word (e.g. *I think it's T-R-O-U – not W –S-E-R-S*) before checking as a class.

> **Answers**   trowsers = trousers   wich = which
> mobail = mobile   brort = brought

2 Students read the story again and work in pairs to answer the questions. Check answers as a class.

> **Answers**   1 in the forest; because it was a cold day
> 2 because they got lost
> 3 glad (that the girl brought her phone)

3 Ask students to look at the three pictures. Ask them, *What can you see in the pictures?* Accept all suitable answers. With a weaker class, write some of the vocabulary on the board, e.g *field, wall, broken, repaired*. Read the exam tip and ask students to answer the three questions about the story in Exercise 1, e.g. *What did the people do?* They went for a walk but they got lost. *Why did the girl use her mobile?* To help them find the way. *How did they feel?* The mother felt glad the girl had her mobile. Then students answer the questions in pairs.

> **Answers**   1 In the countryside. They were walking.
> 2 They saw a farmer. The sheep were leaving the field because the wall was broken. The farmer was upset.
> 3 The teenagers helped the farmer. They repaired the wall and took the sheep back to the field.
> 4 words like *because, and, so, when, then*

☑ Exam task

Students write the story shown in the pictures. Remind them to include the ideas in the exam tip (what the people did, why they did it, how they felt) and their answers from Exercise 3, and also to use linkers (*and, but, so, because and while*) to connect their sentences.

> **Sample answer**
> Some teenagers were walking in the countryside when they saw a farmer. He was upset because he was losing his sheep. A wall was broken and the sheep were walking into a road. The teenagers wanted to help the farmer, so some repaired the wall and the others took the sheep back into the field.

4 Students use the bullet points to check their story. Remind them to check their writing in the exam in the same way. Then students give their story to another student to read and check again.

1 🔊 **37** With books closed, ask students if they have been on an adventure holiday and what activities they did, or what adventure activities they would like to do. Write a list on the board, e.g. rafting, rock climbing, horse riding, sailing, mountain biking. Make sure all the activities in the pictures are listed (horse riding, mountain biking, jumping into a river, sailing). Then, students look at the pictures and listen to the recording to answer the question.

> **Answers**   Luisa talks about pictures 2 and 4. Alexander talks about pictures 1 and 3.

Recording script

Luisa:	This boy is horse riding. I really like horse riding. It's fun and I like horses.
Alexander:	Oh, I don't. I prefer riding bikes. Like this girl. I like mountain biking. It's exciting.
Luisa:	I think this is exciting – jumping into a river from somewhere high.
Alexander:	Mm. But I don't like this activity. The one on the boat. I think sailing is a bit boring.

2 Ask students if they can remember the answer to the two questions. Accept all suggestions. Students listen again to check their answers.

> **Answer**   Alexander doesn't like sailing (picture 3). He thinks it's boring.

3 Students work in pairs to write a list of adjectives for each picture. Check answers as a class and write the words on the board.

> **Answers**   fun, dangerous, exciting, boring, awesome, frightening, challenging

4 🔊 **38** Students listen to identify the words used by Luisa and Alexander, and check whether they are on the board. If they aren't on the board, add them now.

Recording script

Examiner:	Luisa, do you think cycling in the forest is fun?
Luisa:	Yes, maybe, but I don't think I want to try it.
Examiner:	Why?
Luisa:	Because it looks <u>dangerous</u>!
Examiner:	What do you think, Alexander?
Alexander:	I don't agree. I think it looks really <u>exciting</u>. And better than cycling in a city.
Examiner:	Why?
Alexander:	Well, cycling in the city is <u>boring</u>. This looks <u>awesome</u>!
Examiner:	Thank you.

5 Students work in pairs to put the expressions into the table. Check answers as a class.

> **Answers**   Agree: Probably, yes., Yes, I do., Yes, I think it is. Disagree: No, I don't think so., Not really., Not for me., I disagree.

6 Read the exam tip together and tell students that agreeing and disagreeing with their partner is a good way to show that they are listening and following the conversation. Remind students to use the adjectives on the board to express their opinions about the pictures as well as the expressions in Exercise 5 for agreeing and disagreeing.

☑ Exam task

Students should talk about all the pictures in a. They should spend between one and two minutes on a. Then students ask and answer the questions in b. Remind students to listen to their partner's opinion and then agree or disagree with it explaining why. In the exam, the examiner will ask each candidate at least one question to extend the conversation and then a rounding-off question (e.g. *Which of the activities do you like best?*) to end Part 2 Phase 1. Monitor the conversations and make sure that students are using the expressions for agreeing and disagreeing appropriately.

Sample answers

A:	OK, in this first activity, the boy or girl is climbing, maybe a mountain. I have never been climbing, but I would like to. It looks very exciting.
B:	I disagree. Maybe it's exciting, but it is also dangerous. It's not for me. I prefer this picture – walking in the countryside. Do you like it?
A:	Yes, I do. It's very relaxing and it is fun if you use a map. What about this picture – fishing?
B:	Mm. I don't like this activity. It looks lonely and boring because you sit all day in the same place. I prefer swimming because I like exercise. Swimming is fun. But not in a river or lake. It's too cold and dangerous.
A:	I agree about fishing, but I disagree about swimming. I love swimming in a river or lake. And I am interested in this picture too – windsurfing. It looks exciting. What do you think?
B:	No, not for me. It looks difficult and I don't like cold water.

UNIT OBJECTIVES

A2 KEY FOR SCHOOLS TOPICS: health, medicine & illness, personal feelings

GRAMMAR: present perfect, *just, yet & already, for & since*

VOCABULARY: the body, health & illness, adjectives

READING & WRITING PART 2: recognising synonyms;

PART 4: using context to choose answers;

PART 6: identifying and answering questions

LISTENING PART 3: understanding why options are incorrect

SPEAKING PART 1: asking the examiner to say the question again

Health & medicine

Reading & Writing Part 4

STARTER
With books closed, challenge the students to name as many parts of the body as they can. The students will then write down these words in Exercise 3.

1 Pre-teach *grow* and *brush* before the students answer the questions. Don't tell the students the answers. Ask them to read the text in Exercise 2 to find their answers.

> **Answers**   1 b 1.25 cm a month   2 c 2 to 3 minutes

2 Encourage the students to underline the answers in the text. When the students have finished, ask them to tell you what other information they find out.

> **Answers**   1 Most people's hair grows <u>1.25 cm a month</u>.
> 2 Brush them for <u>two to three minutes</u> at least twice a day.

3 Encourage the students to add more parts of the body to the table. Students won't be able to add *hair* because it's uncountable. If the students brainstormed some other parts of the body in the Starter activity, they should also add these. Point out that the plural forms of *foot* and *tooth* are *feet* and *teeth*.

> **Answers**   one: back, neck, stomach, mouth, nose; two: ear, eye, foot, hand, leg; more than two: tooth

Grammar – Present perfect; *just*

4 Exercises 4 and 5 focus on the form of the present perfect. Make sure the students can recognise the present perfect before they look for examples in the text.

> **Answers**   My mum has just cut my hair; I've just been to the dentist; And have you bought a new toothbrush this year? The past participle always comes after *have* or *has* in the present perfect.

5 Point out that some verbs are regular and the past participle form is verb + *-ed* (like the past simple) and other verbs are irregular. Refer the students to the spelling rules for regular verbs in the Grammar reference on page 105. There is an irregular verb table on page 124.

> **Answers**   2 desided = decided   3 eatten = eaten
> 4 wathed = watched   5 attened = attended
> 6 forgetten = forgotten

6 Ask students to look again at the three examples of the present perfect that they underlined in Exercise 4. Point out the different word order in the positive and question forms (*I've just been… / Have you bought …?*). Students do the exercise and compare their answers in pairs. Check answers as a class.

> **Answers**   2 I've lost my tablet.
> 3 Have you finished your homework?
> 4 It hasn't stopped raining all morning.
> 5 Has Sue read the book?

7 Point out that we often use the present perfect to describe an action which happened before now if the action is important in the present (e.g. *He's hurt his foot*) and we use *just* to say we did this a very short time ago. Point out that we use *just* between *have/has* and the past participle: *He's just hurt his foot.*

> **Answers**   2 's just cut / has just cut
> 3 've just had / have just had   4 've just visited / have just visited
> 5 've just brushed / have just brushed

Grammar – *yet / already*

8 Focus attention on the 'To do' list. Explain that Lucas and Saskia are planning a party and the list includes what they have to do. The tick shows they have done that item. Students check their answers in pairs and then as a class.

> **Answers**   2 ✓   3 ✗

9 Ask the students to say which two words mean *before now* (*yet* and *already*) in Exercise 8. Elicit that we normally use *already* for positive sentences and *yet* for negative sentences and questions. Explain *already* normally goes in the middle and *yet* at the end of the sentence. Encourage the students to read the complete email first before writing. Then they should choose *yet* or *already*. Refer students to the Grammar reference on page 105.

> **Answers**   1 already   2 already   3 yet   4 yet

10 Look at the exam task together as a class and ask the students to say what they have to do in this part (read a text and choose the correct answer A, B or C). Read the exam tip as a class. Point out that in this exercise, students have to try to identify the differences between the words in order to decide which word goes with the words before or after the gap in the text. Tell them that they should use this strategy in the exam, too.

> **Answers**   1 / 2 / 3 The answer to all three is 'yes'.
> 4 If you hold a pair of glasses, you have them in your hand. If you wear a pair of glasses, you put them over your eyes. If you take a pair of glasses, you carry them with you somewhere.
> 5 The correct answer to question 1 is B.

☑ Exam task

Encourage the students to read the complete article first without writing and to say what it is about.

> **Answers**   2 A   3 C   4 A   5 B   6 B

CLIL Science: Students work in small groups. Each group chooses another product related to health, for example, the toothbrush or toothpaste, the hearing aid, the walking stick, a hairbrush or soap. They should find information on the internet and write their own short history to present to the rest of the class.

▶ See the Workbook and online resources for further practice.

Health & illness

Reading & Writing Part 2

1 With books closed, brainstorm a list of problems associated with parts of the body, e.g. teeth (*toothache*), back (*backache* or *my back hurts*), head (*headache* or *my head hurts*). Point out that with *ache* we say *I have (a) backache / headache / toothache / stomachache,* etc., and we also say *My head/back/tooth/stomach hurts.* Then encourage the students to think of some possible cures, e.g. *I've got a headache. – You should lie down.* Encourage students to read the conversation before writing.

> **Answers**   2 matter   3 hurts   4 hot   5 temperature   6 down

2 Ask students if they remember what they have to do in this part of the exam. If necessary, they can look at the exam task. (They have to read three short texts and answer seven questions.) Look at the exam tip together and remind students that they need to find other ways of saying some of the words or phrases in the questions. Students do Exercise 2 in pairs. Check answers as a class, making sure students read out the parts of the text they have underlined.

> **Answers**
> 1 F (Maria didn't go to school on Monday. / On Tuesday … her mum said, 'I think you're well enough for school today.'
> 2 F (Her mum thought she probably had a cold.)
> 3 F (She was bored and she missed her friends.)
> 4 F (On Tuesday she felt better.)
> 5 T (Maria was glad.)

☑ Exam task

Tell students to read all the questions before looking for the answers in the texts. Remind them that the words used in the texts will not always be the words used in the questions.

> **Answers**   1 C   2 B   3 A   4 C   5 A   6 B   7 C

Reading & Writing Part 6

Grammar – Present perfect with *for* & *since*

1 Elicit what is the matter with Anya. Point out that the present perfect can also describe an action or situation which started in the past and continues into the present. Refer students to the Grammar reference on page 106.

> **Answers**   1 three days ago   2 yes
> 3 She's afraid of dentists.

2 Looking at the conversation in Exercise 1, students say when we use *for* and *since*: *for* + a period of time and *since* + a point in time. Students keep a list in their notebooks, e.g.

for	since
3 days	9 o'clock
a week, etc.	Tuesday, etc.

Students can add the words in the exercise to their list.

> **Answers**   1 since   2 since   3 for   4 for   5 since

> **FURTHER PRACTICE**
> Students rewrite the sentences so that they are true for them, e.g. *I've had short hair for three years.* Then, in pairs, they ask and answer questions about their sentences using *How long …?*, e.g. *How long have you had short hair? I've had short hair for three years.*

3 Read the exam tip together and point out that students need to focus carefully on each of the three questions given in the Part 6 exam task. This exercise gives students the opportunity to match typical Part 6 questions with appropriate answers. Students do the task in pairs. Check answers as a class.

> **Answers**   1 b   2 e   3 f   4 d   5 a   6 c

4 Remind students that they need to write complete sentences when answering the questions in Part 6, and explain that this exercise will practise this.

☑ Exam task

Ask students to identify the three questions they need to answer. Remind them that they have to write 25 words or more. Encourage students to check their work. Ask two or three students to read their answers to the class.

Sample answer   Dear Robyn,
To keep fit I go swimming at my local pool once a week. I usually go with my friend Jana. We've done it for about three months.
Best wishes,
Marta

Personal feelings

Listening Part 3

1 Encourage the students to look at the faces first and to say the feeling before they read the words.

Answers   2 hungry   3 bored   4 angry   5 sick   6 unhappy

2 Point out there may be different possible answers. Encourage students to compare their answers and feelings.

Sample answers   2 I feel very hungry and a little angry.
3 I feel great and very lucky.   4 I feel sorry.   5 I feel afraid.

FURTHER PRACTICE

Students choose two new words from Exercise 1 and write about a situation when they feel like this. In small groups, the students take turns to read their situation and to say how they feel in each one, e.g. *You've just eaten too many cakes. How do you feel? I feel really sick.*

3 🔊 **39** Ask students to say what they have to do in the exam task (listen to two friends talking and choose the correct answer A–C). Read the exam tip as a class. Point out that the students will hear the other two answers but they should think about why these answers are incorrect.

Answer   The correct answer is C.
A is wrong because she doesn't mention food.
B is wrong because she says Georgia was tired, but she was OK.

Recording script

Joey:	How was your Healthy Living Day, Alissa?
Alissa:	Great! My cousin Georgia and I learned about living in a healthy way, and tried some different sports.
Joey:	Were you tired afterwards?
Alissa:	Georgia was, and she didn't feel well. I was OK but I needed something to drink. I forgot to take anything!

☑ Exam task

🔊 **40** Encourage the students to read the questions and the answers first before they listen. Play the recording twice. Encourage the students to compare their answers and to say why the other two options are incorrect.

Answers   2 A   3 B   4 C   5 C

Recording script

You will hear Alissa talking to her friend Joey about a Healthy Living Day at a sports centre.

Joey:	How was your Healthy Living Day, Alissa?
Alissa:	Great! My cousin Georgia and I learned about living in a healthy way, and tried some different sports.
Joey:	Were you tired afterwards?
Alissa:	Georgia was, and she didn't feel well. I was OK but (1) I needed something to drink. I forgot to take anything!
Joey:	Was it expensive?
Alissa:	No, £20 for adults, and £15 for under 16s. But we're members, (2) so it was only £10 for us.
Joey:	I think I'd like to do a Healthy Living Day.
Alissa:	You! Why?
Joey:	It's different from the things I usually do. All that exercise! (3) I need to do more of that! And if you and Georgia go again, I'll be with friends. When's the next day?
Alissa:	(4) I've booked a place for July 5th but the next one is actually on 28th May. They're always on Saturdays.
Joey:	I'm free most Saturdays after 14th June, so I'll come to the one you booked. Can you do climbing there?
Alissa:	They don't have a wall, unfortunately. (5) I'm going to do hockey, and Georgia wants to try skateboarding.
Joey:	I like Georgia's idea – it sounds the best!

Speaking Part 1 (Phase 1 and 2)

1 Students describe what they can see in the photos. Have a brief discussion on what the students do to keep fit and healthy, e.g. *What do you do to keep fit? Are you a member of a sports club or gym? What do you do to keep healthy? Do you eat well?* Students think of the trainer's questions but they should not write their questions yet.

Sample answers   b What's your surname?
c Where do you live?   d How long have you lived there?
e When were you born?   f What school do you go to?
g What are your favourite sports?
h What's your favourite food?
i Have you got any health problems?
j What do you do in your free time?

2 🔊 **41** Point out that the students will hear the information in order and they will need to spell Brody's surname and the name of his school correctly as the spelling is given. They write the answers on the form.

Answers   2 Madden   3 22 Crawley Street   4 4/four years
5 24 May 2004 / 24/5/2004   6 Petersdale High School
7 hockey and basketball   8 salad, fish and vegetables
9 No   10 meet friends, ride bike, go to the skate park, go to the cinema

Recording script

Trainer: Good morning! I'm Ellie. Before we start, I'd like to ask you some questions, please.

Brody: OK.

Trainer: Now, what's your name?

Brody: It's (1) <u>Brody</u>.

Trainer: And what's your surname, Brody?

Brody: It's Madden.

Trainer: Where do you live?

Brody: I live in Petersdale at (3) <u>22 Crawley Street</u>.

Trainer: And how long have you lived there?

Brody: (4) <u>For about four years, I think</u>.

Trainer: When were you born?

Brody: (5) <u>24th May 2004</u>. Am I too young for the club?

Trainer: No, that's fine. We've got a special programme for kids of your age. What school do you go to?

Brody: (6) <u>I go to Petersdale High School</u>.

Trainer: What sports do you like?

Brody: (7) <u>I like team sports like hockey and basketball</u>.

Trainer: Now, Brody, what's your favourite food?

Brody: (8) <u>I like salad, fish and vegetables best</u>.

Trainer: That sounds healthy! OK, have you got any health problems?

Brody: (9) <u>No</u>, I don't think so.

Trainer: Now the last question … Tell me about your weekend.

Brody: Well, (10) <u>I often get up early on Saturday and meet my friends. We sometimes ride our bikes or go to the skate park. On Saturday afternoon, I sometimes go to the cinema with my family. I love cartoons</u>. On Sunday, I usually stay at home and I do my homework.

Trainer: Thanks, Brody. I think we have the perfect sports programme for you. On Tuesdays, you'll …

3 🔊 **41** With a weaker class, it might be necessary to play the recording several times.

> **Answer**   b) And, what's your surname, Brody?
> c) Where do you live?   d) And how long have you lived there?
> e) When were you born?   f) What school do you go to?
> g) What sports do you like?
> h) Now, Brody, what's your favourite food?
> i) Have you got any health problems?
> j) Tell me about your weekend.

4 🔊 **42** In Speaking Part 1 Phase 1, the examiner will ask personal information questions similar to the types of questions you might ask someone when you meet them for the first time. Point out that in the exam, the examiner will ask questions to each candidate in turn. In this recording, we only hear the examiner and one candidate.

> **Sample answers**   a, b, h, j

Recording script

Examiner: Good morning!

Ariana: Good morning!

Examiner: <u>What's your name?</u>

Ariana: It's Ariana.

Examiner: <u>And what's your surname?</u>

Ariana: It's Rodriquez.

Examiner: Where do you come from?

Ariana: I'm sorry. I don't understand.

Examiner: <u>Where do you live?</u>

Ariana: Sorry. I live in Spain.

Examiner: Do you study English at school?

Ariana: Yes, I do.

Examiner: What subjects do you like best?

Ariana: I like sport.

Examiner: Why?

Ariana: Because I love running and I'm good at it.

Examiner: What's your favourite meal of the day?

Ariana: Can you say that again, please?

Examiner: What's your favourite meal of the day?

Ariana: My favourite meal? I like dinner best, I think.

Examiner: What do you normally have for dinner?

Ariana: We often have soup or salad.

Examiner: Who usually cooks in your house?

Ariana: My mum or my dad, or sometimes I cook.

Examiner: <u>Tell me about your weekend</u>.

Ariana: Well, I often go running on Saturday morning with my dad. In the afternoon, I meet my friends and we go to the town centre. On Sunday, we sometimes have lunch at my grandmother's house.

Examiner: Thank you, Ariana.

5 🔊 **42** Read the exam tip as a class. Make sure the students can pronounce the expressions well.

> **Answers**   Sorry?   I'm sorry. I don't understand.
> Can you say that again, please?

✓ Exam task

Remind the students to use the expressions *I'm sorry, Pardon?* etc. if they don't understand. For more Speaking Part 1 practice, see the Speaking bank on page 63.

> **Suggested answers**
> **Student A:**   Good morning!
> **Student B:**   Good morning!
> **Student A:**   What's your name?
> **Student B:**   It's Faruk.
> **Student A:**   And what's your surname?
> **Student B:**   It's Demir.
> **Student A:**   How do you spell that?
> **Student B:**   I'm sorry. I don't understand.
> **Student A:**   How do you spell that?
> **Student B:**   Ah! It´s D-E-M-I-R.
> **Student A:**   Where do you live?
> **Student B:**   I live in Turkey.
> **Student A:**   Tell me about your weekend.
> **Student B:**   I often play basketball on Saturday morning with my team. In the afternoon, I meet my friends and we ride our bikes or we go swimming. On Sunday, we usually have lunch with my aunt and cousins.
> **Student A:**   Thank you.

UNIT OBJECTIVES

A2 KEY FOR SCHOOLS TOPICS: communication, appliances

GRAMMAR: the passive, present and past simple, passive or active

VOCABULARY: communication, describing objects

READING & WRITING PART 2: underlining key words; **PART 5:** identifying the type of missing word

LISTENING PART 5: using context clues to choose the correct answers

SPEAKING PART 2: making comparisons to say which is better

Communication

Listening Part 5

STARTER

Write *I couldn't live without my … because* on the board, checking comprehension. Explain that you want students to complete the sentence about a piece of technology. Model an example sentence. Then put students in groups to discuss their ideas, before opening it up to the class. Use the board to write down any interesting language / errors you hear from the students.

1 Encourage the students to look at the photo first and to say what they can see.

> **Answer** A PC Bang is a kind of internet café or games centre where you can meet your friends and play computer games.

2 With a weaker class, write the verbs on the board in the wrong order first to help the students.

> **Answers** 1 use 2 spend 3 send 4 posted
> 5 downloaded 6 play

3 In pairs, students ask and answer the questions for themselves. Monitor, making sure they are answering in full sentences and giving more information where possible.

4 🔊 **43** Read through the exam tip and explain how words like but, *instead* and now can help students decide on a correct answer. Model an example sentence on the board: *Mike used to use his tablet for the internet but now*

he uses his phone. Ask students how Mike accesses the internet (his phone - he used his tablet in the past). You could model similar examples for *but* and *instead* (e.g. *I did have a games console <u>but</u> it broke, so now I play games on my laptop; I don't watch DVDs any more. I watch online <u>instead</u>.*) to show how the audio might 'trick' students into choosing a wrong answer.

Ask students to listen and tick the things the friends got new (emphasising the word *new*) but pointing out that for each person they will hear both things mentioned. Play the recording. Students check their answers with a partner. Check as a class after the second listening. You might want to give students the audioscript so they can see the answers in each case and check why each answer is correct.

> **Answers** 2 Elsa: printer 3 Callum: DVD
> 4 Sunita: games console

> **Recording script**
>
> **Brother:** I've just seen Leo. He's got a new mobile phone.
>
> **Susie:** No, he hasn't. It's his brother's but (1) <u>his laptop is new</u>. Have you seen it?
>
> **Brother:** No, I haven't. It was his sister's birthday yesterday. What did she get?
>
> **Susie:** Who, Elsa? (2) <u>She usually asks for DVDs but this year she got a printer</u>.
>
> **Brother:** Cool! And what about your friend Callum? Has he spent his birthday money yet?
>
> **Susie:** Yes, he has. (3) <u>He wanted to buy a games console but he bought a DVD instead</u>.
>
> **Brother:** Really? We've got an old games console he can have.
>
> **Susie:** That's true. (4) <u>My friend Sunita has just bought a new games console</u>. It's amazing! You can even watch DVDs on it.

5 Students read the exam task and compare answers in pairs before checking as a class.

> **Answers** Tasha is talking to a friend. She is talking about her family and each person's favourite thing.

✓ Exam task

🔊 **44** Students say what they have to do in this task (listen to Tasha and match the people 1–5 with their favourite thing A–H). Read the exam tip as a class. Remind students that Tasha will talk about each member of the family in order. She may mention two of the things for each person but only one will be their favourite thing. Play the recording twice.

> **Answers** 1 B 2 H 3 E 4 D 5 F

For each question, choose the correct answer. You will hear Tasha talking to a friend about her family. What is each person's favourite thing?

Boy: Hi, Tasha. What's the matter?

Tasha: (0) <u>I've broken my dad's CD player and it's his favourite thing.</u>

Boy: Wow! I didn't know people still used CD players!

Tasha: Dad does! My family is so old-fashioned. (1) <u>Mum has only just bought a digital camera. And now she likes it more than anything else.</u> She uses my laptop to look at the photos!

Boy: But your sister has a laptop too! I suppose that's her favourite thing.

Tasha: Well, she plays games on it but (2) <u>I think she prefers the TV.</u> She spends hours watching it.

Boy: Is your brother's tablet still his favourite thing?

Tasha: Now (3) <u>it's the mobile he got for his birthday.</u>

Boy: What did he do with the tablet?

Tasha: He gave it to our grandma so she could use the internet. (4) <u>Then she was given a laptop. She says that's her favourite thing because it's bigger.</u> She speaks to my cousins in Australia on it.

Boy: Does your grandfather still borrow DVDs from the library?

Tasha: He doesn't need to. We taught him how to download films onto the PC that he never used before and now (5) <u>he says it's the best thing in the world!</u>

Grammar – The passive: present simple

6 Ask students if the pictures are true for them. After the students have answered the questions, elicit how we form the passive (object + *be* + past participle + *by* subject) and when we use it, i.e. when we do not know who or what does the action or when we are not interested in who or what does or did the action. Refer the students to the Grammar reference on page 107 if necessary.

> **Answers**   1 Yes, his friends.
> 2 No, we don't and it isn't important.   3 Sentence 2.
> 4 We form the passive with *be* + the past participle.

7 Encourage the students to complete the sentences first. Remind them to use the correct form of *be* in each sentence, e.g. 2 *Films are* but 3 *This is*. Then check they understand the meaning of the words in the box.

> **Answers**   2 are watched; screen   3 is needed; keyboard
> 4 is downloaded; internet
> 5 is moved, is clicked / 's clicked; mouse
> 6 are sent; email address.

8 Invite a brief class discussion about Instagram before the students do this exercise: *What is it? How many of you use it? Who can see your photos and videos?* Students read the complete text first before writing.

> **Answers**   1 is used   2 is downloaded
> 3 isn't used / is not used   4 aren't called / are not called
> 5 're known / are known   6 are followed

FURTHER PRACTICE

Write these skeleton questions on the board:

1   you / send / more than 20 messages a day?

2   all your homework / do / on a computer?

3   your computer / turn on for most of the day?

4   you / give / computer games, programs, books, etc. for your birthday?

5   your favourite webpage / make / by you?

6   most of your clothes and books / buy / online?

In pairs, students write complete questions using the passive. Then, they take turns to ask and answer the questions.

> **Answers**   1 Are you sent more than 20 messages a day?
> 2 Is all your homework done on a computer?
> 3 Is your computer turned on for most of the day?
> 4 Are you given computer games, programs, books, etc. for your birthday?
> 5 Is your favourite webpage made by you?
> 6 Are most of your clothes and books bought online?

▶ *See the Workbook and online resources for further practice.*

Reading & Writing Part 2

1 Invite a brief class discussion about what ICT is and whether the students study it at school.

> **Sample answer**   Yes, we study ICT at school. We do it on Monday and Wednesday.

2 Ask the students to look at the exam task and to say what they have to do: read three short paragraphs about three different people and answer seven questions. The answers to the questions are the names of the three different people. Ask the students what the exam task is about (three young people talking about technology). Read the exam tip as a class.

> **Sample answers**
> 1 *A Berta* is the correct answer; she says *We also do ICT every Wednesday.*
> 2 *C Gloria* is not the correct answer because she says *We don't study ICT as a school subject.*

3 Read the exam tip and point out that in this kind of task, the words are not difficult vocabulary but common words in English grammar. Point out that prepositions (which students saw in the previous exercise) are often missing words in this kind of task. Then ask the students to look at the exercise in pairs and match the example words in the box to the part of speech category.

> **Answers**   1 A   2 A   3 B   4 C   5 B   6 B   7 C

✓ Exam task

Encourage students to read the paragraphs before they answer the questions. They should underline the important words in the questions and the answers in the paragraphs. Remind them not to choose an answer because the same words are in the paragraph. Students compare their answers by saying, e.g. *I think ... is correct because in the paragraph it says ... .*

Answers	2 A 3 B 4 C 5 B 6 B 7 C

CLIL ICT/Maths: In small groups, students design a technology questionnaire to find out how their classmates use technology at school and at home and what they think schools and homes will be like in the future. Give the students some example questions but encourage the groups to write some of their own, e.g. *1 Do you use digital books or interactive whiteboards at school? 2 What will smart schools be like in the future? 3 Will we still have teachers in classrooms in the future? 4 How will artificial intelligence (AI) be used in homes and schools in the future?* Students use a web tool like Survey Monkey to create their questionnaire and then encourage their classmates to complete it. Each group should then present their results to the class using spreadsheet software like Microsoft Excel to produce graphs, charts and diagrams to illustrate the results, etc.

Grammar

Grammar – The passive: past simple

1 Encourage the students to look at the pictures and to say what the objects are before they read the sentences (A laptop computer, B Walkman, C telephone). When the students have finished the exercise, ask them to underline the verb forms. Elicit that these are all examples of the past simple passive. If necessary, refer the students to the Grammar reference on page 107.

Answers	A 2 B 1 C 3

2 With books closed, ask students *How do you get news and messages?* Elicit different ways, e.g. mobile phone, TV, the internet. Ask them to try and say in what order these things were invented. With books open, the students check their ideas and write complete sentences like the example. Remind the students to use the past passive.

Answers	2 The first person was phoned in 1876.
	3 TVs were watched for the first time in 1925.
	4 The internet was used for the first time in 1969.

FURTHER PRACTICE

In small groups, students research the history of a piece of technology or service, e.g. the iPod or MP3 player, the mobile phone, the internet, messaging. They then use a web tool like Timetoast to create an online history timeline. If possible, they should include some sentences in the passive.

3 Point out that these sentences are in both the present and past passive. There may be mistakes with the form (*writed* instead of *written*) or the use (present instead of past).

Answers	2 it made = it is made
	3 was writed = was written 4 broke = was broken
	5 gave = was given 6 is made = was made

4 Remind students when we use the passive by writing two example sentences on the board and asking questions, e.g.

1 I love watching films. (Who loves watching films? I do) ACTIVE

2 I'm often given DVDs for my birthday. (Who gives her the DVDs? We don't know.) PASSIVE

Encourage the students to read the complete conversation before they choose the correct answers.

Answers	1 was woken 2 did she do 3 was given
	4 decided 5 was sent 6 Do you want 7 love 8 isn't called

Speaking Part 2 (Phase 2)

1 🔊 **45** Before they do the exercise, ask students how they listen to music and what other ways of listening to music they know about. Write a list on the board. After listening, ask students if the answers to question 1 are on the board. A weaker class can listen to the recording more than once.

Answers
1 record player, download from the internet, CDs
2 Deniz thinks downloaded music sounds best.

Recording script	
Silvia:	What's that, Deniz?
Deniz:	(1) It's a record player. It's what people listened to music on before you could download music or buy CDs.
Silvia:	Why do you like it?
Deniz:	I like collecting the records. They're really cool, and some are different colours.
Silvia:	But what about the music? How does it sound?
Deniz:	(2) Well, maybe not as good as a download from the internet, but I still like it.

2 Go over the exam tip as a class. Tell students to listen to the recording again to focus on an example of how to make a comparison. If necessary, tell students the extract in the exercise is at the end of the recording.

Answers	as … as

3 Write two sentences on the board using (not) as … as, e.g. *Maria is **as tall as** Anna, This classroom is **not as big as** the computer room.* Underline (not) as + adjective + as and explain the meaning (two things are the same / different). Elicit other examples from the class. Students then complete the sentences and compare their answers with a partner.

Answers	1 fast 2 big 3 fun 4 dark 5 heavy
	6 interesting

4 Encourage students to use *as … as* and *not as … as* to answer the questions, e.g. *I prefer watching films on my laptop because my phone is not as big as my laptop.*

✅ Exam task

Ask students if they can remember the language to use if they don't understand the examiner's questions. Write the phrases on the board for a weaker group (*I'm sorry, I don't understand. Pardon? Sorry? Can you say that again, please?*). The students listen to the examiner's questions with their books closed. Remind students to make comparisons in their answers.

Sample answers
1 A: Do you prefer phoning people, or sending messages? Why?
   B: I prefer phoning people. I like sending messages when I can't speak to the person, but I think phoning people is better because it is often faster than messaging.
2 B: Do you like using your phone to take photos? Why? / Why not?
   A: Yes, I do. It's very convenient because I always have my phone so I can take photos anywhere and it is easy to show other people or to share or upload using my phone.
3 A: Is it better to play computer games alone, or with other people?
   B: It depends. Some games are only for one person so I play those games alone. But I also play some multi-player games online and this is fun because you are playing with your friends and you can speak to them during the game.

Appliances

Reading & Writing Part 5

1 Students look at the pictures first and say what they can see before they read the sentences. Remind the students to count the number of gaps to see how many letters are missing. Check they spell these words correctly.

Answers	2 case 3 lamp 4 washing machine
	5 fridge 6 cooker

2 Encourage the students to underline the examples of *made of, by* and *in* in the descriptions in Exercise 1 and to say when we use each one before they match 1–3 with a–c.

Answers	1c 2a 3b

3 Ask the students to look at the Reading & Writing Part 5 exam task and say what they have to do (read two emails and write one word for each gap). Point out that in some exam tasks (as in Unit 6), there is one email but in others, as here, there are two emails. Read the exam tip as a class. Remind the students that they should look at the subject of the sentence (*I, you, he,* etc.), the tense (present, past, future) and, if it is a verb with two parts, the part given (e.g. *Today I …. wearing* or *Did you …. to the park yesterday?*).

Answers	1 their; us 2 an; the 3 but; so 4 have; will
	5 ago; since; soon

✅ Exam task

Encourage the students to read both emails first and to say what the problem is in the first email (Baha's lost his phone) and what the response is in the second (the phone has been found). Remind the students that they should only write ONE word in each gap and that their spelling of these words MUST be correct.

Answers	1 was 2 a 3 you 4 in 5 has 6 when / if

▶ *See the Workbook and online resources for further practice.*

Photocopiable resources

Unit 1

Recording script

You will hear Simon talking to his friend Amanda about his school day. Now listen to the conversation.

Amanda: Hi, Simon! How are you?

Simon: Oh hi, Amanda! I'm tired!

Amanda: Me too! I go to sleep really late because my brother watches TV in his room, and I can hear it.

Simon: Oh, that's a shame! But you don't have to get up really early, like I do!

Amanda: Get up really early? Why's that?

Simon: I take the boat to school now. It goes at half past seven, so Mum wakes us up at a quarter past six. We have breakfast and leave home at seven.

Amanda: So you've changed schools?

Simon: Yes. The school on our island is for six to eleven year olds. Now I'm twelve, I go to school on another island with my sister Tanya. She's fourteen now.

Amanda: Oh. What about getting home?

Simon: The boat goes two hours after school finishes. Mum's sister lives near the school so we have dinner there.

Amanda: So that's your school day! It's not like mine – much more interesting – and longer!

Simon: It's what everyone my age on the island does.

Amanda: Some people probably think it's fun, or even exciting, but I don't like boats.

Simon: Well, it's the only way!

Unit 2

Recording script

1 You will hear two friends talking about a film they've just seen. What type of film was it?

Boy: I really liked that film.

Girl: Me too! Usually I prefer adventure stories, and I've never liked scary films before, but that one was great – really enjoyable.

Boy: I know! It's strange, isn't it, that we think it's fun to be frightened.

Girl: Yeah, that's funny, isn't it? But we only like it when we know it's not real.

2 You will hear a boy talking about a camping trip. Who did he go camping with?

We had a great time camping. The weather was good, so my uncle and I cooked outside every day. His cooking isn't as good as my mum's, but it's OK. Because it was sunny during the day, it was still quite warm at night, too. I'm lucky – I've never been camping when it's rainy. My brother has. He says it's awful!

3 You will hear a boy, James, talking to his mother about basketball lessons. What does James ask his mother to do?

Mum: Did you see the information about your basketball lessons, James?

James: Yeah – thanks for booking those, Mum. I read the information so I know when the lessons start.

Mum: Yes – next week! Do you need new T-shirts and shorts?

James: Mm. I have some shorts, but they're a bit tight. Can you get me some new ones?

Mum: Yes, I'll do that tomorrow.

4 You will hear two friends discussing a practice for their dance group. What do they still need to do?

Boy: Is everything ready for dance practice tomorrow?

Girl: Nearly. I've downloaded a video of the dance we chose on my phone.

Boy: Great! We picked a good one! Mr. Davies has agreed that we can use the hall, so we have somewhere to dance.

Girl: Good. One more thing – I'm not sure if everyone knows what time to come.

Boy: OK. I'll send a message.

5 You will hear a girl talking about horse riding. Why does she like horse riding?

Girl: I started horse riding last year. I didn't really know anything about horses before, but my friend goes riding, and she invited me to go with her. I go regularly now. It's really fun. It's great to be out in the countryside, in the fresh air – much better than being in a sports centre.

Unit 4

2 *How much was Jenny's new tennis racket?*

Boy: I love your new tennis shoes, Jenny. Were they expensive?

Jenny: No, they weren't. They were £35. My racket was more expensive.

Boy: Oh really? How much was that?

Jenny: I bought it online for £40. My sister paid £45 for hers.

3 *What time does the hockey match start?*

Girl: Excuse me. What time does the hockey match start?

Man: It starts at half past four.

Girl: What time is it now? Am I late?

Man: No, it's only ten past four. Go for a walk and come back at twenty past four.

4 *What is the boy drinking?*

Girl: I'm thirsty after that race.

Simon: This lemonade is really good. I bought it over there in the café.

Girl: Is there any juice?

Simon: I don't think so, but they've got hot chocolate if you prefer that.

5 *Who is the girl's table tennis coach?*

Maisie: That's my table tennis coach.

Boy: Who? Is he that blond man over there with glasses?

Maisie: No, he's got dark hair and he doesn't wear glasses.

Boy: Oh, I can see him now. He's standing over there next to Brendan.

Unit 6

You will hear Ethan and his mum talking about his birthday party. How will each person travel to the party?

Ethan: I'm home!

Mum: Hi, Ethan! I'm in the kitchen. Happy Birthday!

Ethan: Thanks, Mum! But where is everybody? Why are they so late for my party?

Mum: Well, your sister has football practice until 6.00 p.m. Then she's coming home by bus.

Ethan: Why doesn't she take the tram? It's faster. And where's Dad?

Mum: He phoned to say Grandma missed the half past five bus so he's going to drive her.

Ethan: Is Granddad coming in Dad's car, too?

Mum: He had to work this afternoon so he's going to take the underground. It's quicker than the car, anyway.

Ethan: I can hear a motorbike. Is that Uncle Tom?

Mum: I spoke to him this morning. He's going to take a taxi after his meeting.

Ethan: Is Ursula coming with him? Or is she taking the underground?

Mum: Your cousin Ursula's cycling here right now. She'll be here in ten minutes.

Ethan: Great! Who else is coming?

Mum: Your Aunt May!

Ethan: Oh. She'll come by train, won't she?

Mum: Actually, there's a tram where she lives now, so she's getting that. It's nearer than the train.

Ethan: OK. I hope they all get here soon!

Revision answer key

Unit 1

1 1 Have you got / 've got
2 Has Manuela got / hasn't / 's got
3 Have your parents got / they haven't / 's got / 's got
4 Have you got / haven't   5 hasn't got / 've got

2 1 grandmother   2 parents   3 daughter   4 husband
5 cousin   6 wife   7 brother   8 children

3 1 do   2 doesn't walk   3 go   4 plays   5 does
6 doesn't do   7 start   8 watch

4 1 dark   2 tall   3 long   4 curly   5 short   6 straight

Unit 2

1 1 My mum often takes photos of us.

2 My best friend usually draws pictures of animals at art club.

3 I'm sometimes late for my music classes.

4 I go to the cinema with my cousins twice a month.

5 My friends do after-school activities every day.

6 We never sleep in a tent in winter.

2 1 would you like to go / 'd like to go / like swimming

2 do you like listening / like listening

3 Would you like to come / like going

4 would you like to watch / 'd like to watch

5 do you like to / like playing

6 Do you like eating / 'd like to go

3 1 cooking   2 going to concerts   3 dancing
4 messaging friends   5 reading books
6 trying new food   7 playing computer games
8 spending time with friends

Unit 3

1 1 cupboard   2 mirror   3 light / lamp   4 sofa   5 desk
6 bed   7 fridge   8 cooker

2 1 some   2 are/some   3 a   4 is   5 any   6 an   7 some
8 any

3 1 don't have to   2 have to   3 have to   4 don't have to
5 Do you have to   6 doesn't have to   7 have to
8 has to

Unit 4

1 1 writing   2 repairing   3 deciding   4 carrying
5 listening   6 studying   7 playing   8 running

2 1 trainers   2 costume   3 helmet   4 socks   5 skirt
6 jeans   7 T-shirt   8 coat

3 1 does   2 don't understand   3 go   4 is doing
5 comes / speaks   6 do you go   7 is working / wants
8 is winning

4 1 goes   2 play   3 plays   4 do   5 go   6 to go
7 is doing   8 go / going

Unit 5

1 1 enjoyed   2 visited   3 saw   4 went   5 borrowed
6 bought   7 played   8 arrived

2 1 sports centre   2 cinema   3 bookshop   4 pharmacy
5 library   6 department store   7 theatre   8 university

3 1 was / years   2 Did   3 didn't go   4 did you do   5 Was
6 left / minutes   7 didn't like   8 learned / ago

4 1 was / on   2 didn't play / at   3 did (you) do / in
4 weren't / at   5 opened / on   6 Did (you) have / on
7 didn't work / in   8 began / in

Unit 6

1 1 helicopter   2 coach   3 lorry   4 tram   5 ship
6 motorbike   7 taxi   8 boat

2 1 older   2 faster   3 hotter
4 more expensive   5 easier   6 noisier
7 farther/further   8 healthier

3 1 the most difficult   2 the quietest   3 the oldest
4 the worst   5 the most crowded   6 the cheapest

4 1 ride   2 on   3 plane   4 sail   5 crossing   6 drive
7 by   8 bridges

Unit 7

1 1 English   2 geography   3 history   4 art/art history
5 science/geography   6 music   7 maths

2 1 study   2 teach   3 spends   4 miss   5 taking   6 pass

3 1 well   2 easily   3 badly   4 quickly   5 carefully
6 quietly

4 1 can't 2 must 3 mustn't 4 shouldn't 5 can
6 can 7 couldn't 8 could

Unit 8

1 1 have a rest 2 stay at a campsite 3 stay with a family
4 try new dishes 5 stay at home 6 learn a language
7 explore the city

2 1 Were your classmates speaking 2 I was having
3 Were you talking
4 Carla wasn't sleeping / was watching
5 My dad was making 6 It wasn't raining
7 Were you having 8 My mum was reading

3 1 brilliant 2 funny 3 bored 4 tiring 5 exciting

4 1 was riding 2 saw 3 wanted 4 ran 5 saw
6 arrived 7 told 8 was looking 9 told

Unit 9

1 1 're going to the circus / Are (you) going to ask
2 'm going to play / 'm not going to do
3 is/'s going to play / Is (he) going to play
4 're going to watch / 'm going to study
5 Are you going to take / 's not going to rain
6 Are you going to come / 'm going to do

2 1 to visit 2 to take 3 to choose 4 climbing
5 to pass 6 to be 7 learning 8 seeing

3 1 quiz show 2 play 3 the weather
4 music programme 5 the news 6 sports programme

4 1 singer 2 actor 3 dancer 4 artist
5 photographer 6 drummer 7 musician 8 writer

Unit 10

1 1 won't 2 may 3 will 4 may 5 will 6 will 7 may

2 1 wood 2 river 3 field 4 path 5 spring 6 hill
7 gate

3 1 storm 2 ice 3 rain 4 wind 5 sun 6 fog 7 snow

4 1 'll be / don't leave 2 rains / won't go
3 will you do / don't pass
4 will get / don't remember 5 go / will you come
6 don't go / ' ll be 7 will be / don't come
8 miss / will you get

Unit 11

1 1 arm 2 neck 3 hand 4 tooth 5 back 6 face
7 hair

2 1 've passed 2 've never been 3 has fallen
4 have you known 5 haven't decided
6 haven't played 7 hasn't finished 8 Have you eaten

3 1 yet 2 since 3 yet 4 just 5 yet 6 for 7 already
8 yet

4 1 thirsty 2 tired 3 sorry 4 hot 5 hungry 6 sick
7 angry 8 happy

Unit 12

1 1 My shoes are made of leather.
2 I am given money for my birthday.
3 Rugby isn't / is not played at my school.
4 English is spoken all over the world.
5 CDs aren't / are not sold here any more.
6 My brother is called Kieran.

2 1 was made 2 was written 3 was used 4 was won
5 was taught 6 were given

3 1 use 2 send 3 play 4 mobile 5 address
6 download 7 alarm 8 online

4 1 fridge 2 washing machine 3 lamp 4 case
5 screen 6 laptop

Grammar reference answer key

Unit 1

have got and present simple

1 **1** hasn't **2** have **3** have **4** Have / haven't **5** have

2 **1** 've/have got **2** hasn't / has not got **3** 's/has got
4 Have / got / haven't / have not (got it)
5 haven't / have not got

Present simple: be

1 **2** isn't **3** I'm not **4** aren't **5** We're **6** She's

2 **1** is/'s **2** am/'m **3** are **4** Is / isn't / is not / is/'s
5 Are / am

Other verbs in the present simple

1 **1** plays **2** get up **3** likes **4** live **5** goes

2 **1** Lucas doesn't / does not play the piano every evening.
2 I don't / do not get up at nine o'clock at the weekend.
3 My brother doesn't / does not like football.
4 My friends don't / do not live near me.
5 Hannah doesn't / does not go to school by bus.

3 **2** Does your mum get home at 4 p.m. every day? Yes, she does. / No, she doesn't.

3 Do they walk to school on Tuesdays? Yes, they do. / No, they don't.

4 Does he start school at 8.45? Yes, he does. / No, he doesn't.

5 Do you have breakfast every day? Yes, I do. / No, I don't.

4 **1** ~~work~~ works **2** ~~don't~~ doesn't **3** ~~plays~~ play
4 ~~starts~~ start **5** ~~doesn't~~ don't

Question words

1 **1** Where **2** What time / When **3** When **4** How
5 What **6** Who

Unit 2

Adverbs of frequency

1 **1** I never go to school in the evening.
2 My parents sometimes help me with my homework.
3 My brother and I walk to school every day.
4 I am sometimes late for school.
5 I always work hard at school.

2 Students' own answers.

Do you like ...? / Would you like ...?

1 **1** Do **2** Would / to come / love **3** Do **4** Would
5 Would / can't **6** Do

Unit 3

There is/are, a/an, some & any, (don't) have to

1 **1** an **2** There are **3** any/some **4** Some **5** some
6 any **7** There's / There is **6** Are

(don't) have to

1 **1** have to help **2** do you have to do **3** have to tidy
4 Does she have to tidy **5** she does **6** have to do
7 don't have to do

2 **1** have to **2** don't have to **3** don't have to **4** have to
5 have to

Unit 4

Present continuous

1 **1** are not / aren't watching / are/'re listening
2 am/'m writing
3 Are you doing / am/'m not / am/'m playing
4 is/'s running **5** isn't/is not washing

2 **1** ~~readding~~ reading **2** ~~puting~~ putting
3 ~~cookeing~~ cooking **4** ~~siting~~ sitting
5 ~~dancing~~ dancing

Present continuous vs. present simple

1 **1** go **2** is doing **3** love **4** 's starting **5** play **6** have

2 **1** ~~we are usually getting~~ we usually get

2 ~~Listen~~ I'm listening / I am listening **3** ~~is hating~~ hates

4 ~~is having~~ has **5** ~~has~~ is having

6 ~~Do you understanding~~ Do you understand

Unit 5

Irregular verbs

1 1 were / broke / had to 2 did / have / ate / drank
3 did / get / got / gave 4 Did / go / did / went
5 Did / watch / didn't / did not / took / was
6 came / weren't / were not / was

2 1 left 2 won / felt 3 made 4 met / bought 5 began

Time expressions: *in/at/on*

1 1 on 2 at 3 on 4 in 5 in 6 at

2 1 ~~in~~ on 2 ~~on~~ at 3 ~~on~~ in 4 ~~in~~ at 5 ~~on~~ in 6 ~~in~~ at

Unit 6

Comparative & superlative adjectives

1 1 bigger 2 more interesting 3 heavier 4 warmer
5 worse 6 larger

2 1 the most 2 largest 3 worst 4 happiest 5 biggest
6 best

3 1 ~~better~~ best 2 ~~happyer~~ happier 3 ~~fiter~~ fitter
4 ~~the more~~ the most 5 ~~largerer~~ larger
6 ~~taller his~~ taller than his

Unit 7

Modals: *must / mustn't*

1 1 mustn't be 2 must wear 3 mustn't run
4 mustn't talk 5 mustn't use 6 must finish

2 1 You must visit / go to 2 You mustn't use
3 You must try / go to 4 You mustn't lose/forget
5 You must see / visit / go to

Modals: *should / shouldn't*

1 You should … Go to bed early. / Ask your parents or
friends to help you.

You shouldn't … Study late the day before. / Spend too
much time alone. / Worry.

2 1 should drink 2 should wear 3 shouldn't eat
4 shouldn't ride 5 should get 6 shouldn't arrive

Modals: *can/could*

1 1 can't 2 can 3 can't 4 couldn't / could 5 Can /
can't

2 2 Could you swim when you were three?
Yes, I could. / No, I couldn't.

3 Can you speak more than two languages?
Yes, I can. / No, I can't.

4 Can you play basketball?
Yes, I can. / No, I can't.

5 Can both of your parents drive?
Yes, they can. / No, they can't.

Adverbs of manner

1 1 carefully 2 magically 3 early 4 comfortably
5 well 6 beautifully

Unit 8

Past continuous

2 What were you doing last night at ten o'clock?

3 It wasn't raining this morning.

4 I was having a French lesson while they were having an
exam.

5 Sophie wasn't travelling on the bus at 8 a.m.

6 While Jack was reading Emily was playing the guitar.

Past simple & past continuous

1 1 was sleeping / phoned 2 was doing
3 woke up / was raining 4 were you doing

2 2 were travelling 3 were watching 4 were listening
5 saw 6 was standing 7 was telling 8 was coming
9 was

Unit 9

be going to: positive & negative

1 1 are/'re going to miss 2 are/'re going to ride
3 am/'m going to do 4 aren't / 're not going to need
5 are going to visit

2 2 A: What are you going to do this evening?
B: I'm / I am going to play a video game.

3 A: Is it going to rain tomorrow?
B: No, it's / it is going to be sunny all day.

4 A: What are you going to do when you leave school?
B: I'm / I am going to look for a job in a sports centre.

5 A: Is your team going to win the match?
B: No, the other team is much better. We're / We are
going to lose.

Infinitives & -ing forms

1 1 to help 2 playing 3 watching 4 playing
5 helping

2 1 visiting to visit 2 to meet meeting 3 hearing to hear
4 watch watching 5 to wait waiting

Unit 10

will / won't & may

1 Tom and Julie are going. The others are not sure.

2 1 may not have 2 will/'ll go 3 Will / be / won't
4 may get 5 won't pass / will/'ll be 5 will/'ll meet

3 1 We'll probably go to Spain for our holiday next year.

2 I think it will be colder tomorrow.

3 Perhaps we'll have a new teacher next term.

4 Are you sure you'll be OK?

5 He probably won't come to our party.

First conditional

1 1 see / 'll/will tell 2 'll/will hurt / fall
3 don't/do not catch / 'll/will have
4 'll/will be / don't/do not leave 5 is / won't / will not
hear

2 1 If I get a holiday job, I'll earn some money.

2 I'll buy a bike if I have enough money.

3 If I have a bike I'll use it to go to school.

4 I'll get fit if I ride my bike to school.

5 If I don't have enough money for a bike, I'll go to school
by bus.

6 I won't get fit if I go to school by bus.

Unit 11

Present perfect: just/yet/already

1 1 Have you tidied your bedroom yet?

2 They've already finished their school project.

3 I'm really hot. I've just run home from school.

4 I don't want to watch that programme. I've already
seen it twice.

5 Tania doesn't want to go to bed yet. She isn't tired.

2 1 I haven't worn my new shoes yet.

2 We've just finished eating.

3 I've already texted all my friends.

4 Have you finished reading that book yet?

5 I've just phoned my older brother.

Present perfect with for & since

1

For	Since
24 hours	six o'clock
400 years	last November
ten minutes	my birthday
three weeks	October 12th
12 months	the end of May
	yesterday

2 1 two weeks 2 since 3 last week 4 yesterday
5 for 6 the age of nine

Unit 12

The passive: present simple

1 1 is/'s grown 2 are sold 3 are shown 4 is/'s made
5 is/'s closed

The passive: past simple

1 1 was built 2 were told 3 were closed 4 was given
5 were taken 6 was sent

Writing bank answer key

How to make your writing better: adjectives

1

1b There was a comfortable chair in the corner of the room.

2b We had lunch in a small, friendly restaurant.

3b A kind woman showed me the way home.

4b I knew I had made a big mistake.

2

1 true   **2** false   **3** true

3

1 heavy   **4** lovely
2 important   **5** expensive
3 modern/lovely

4

1 exciting, funny
2 beautiful, lovely
3 brilliant, great
4 friendly, kind
5 sunny, pleasant
6 great, excellent

5

1 wonderful   **4** horrible
2 terrible   **5** awful
3 amazing   **6** fantastic

very good	very bad
wonderful	terrible
amazing	horrible
fantastic	awful

How to make your writing better: adverbs and interesting verbs

1

1b I quickly ran home.

2b The children were playing happily in the garden.

3b I read the invitation carefully.

4b She opened the letter slowly.

5b I couldn't see well because it was cloudy.

2

1 true   **3** false
2 true   **4** true

3

1 loudly   **5** carefully
2 hungrily **6** easily
3 clearly   **7** well
4 fast   **8** beautifully

4

1 The police officer spoke to me angrily.

2 I quickly read the letter.

3 She closed the door quietly.

4 He carefully carried the hot drinks into the sitting room.

5 We walked slowly through the park.

6 Mark didn't sleep well last night.

5

1 hurried   **4** jumped
2 shouting **5** threw
3 relaxing **6** cried

6

1 ran   **4** jumped
2 shouted **5** threw
3 relaxed

Use verb forms correctly to talk about the past, present and future

1

Hi Jo,

I <u>go</u> swimming next Saturday. My cousin <u>are</u> here at the moment, and he <u>love</u> swimming. <u>Are you want</u> to come too? There's a swimming pool on Wood Road. We can <u>to</u> get the bus. I <u>meet</u> you at the bus stop.

Sam

2

Hi Jo,

I <u>will go</u> swimming next Saturday. My cousin is here at the moment, and he <u>loves</u> swimming. <u>Do you want</u> to come too? There's a swimming pool on Wood Road. We <u>can get</u> the bus. I will <u>meet</u> you at the bus stop.

Sam

3

1 'm going   **5** 've never been
2 is   **6** went
3 loves   **7** get
4 Do you want **8** can meet

4

1 'm going
2 went
3 've never been
4 We can get, I can meet

5

1 'm going   **4** to come
2 bought   **5** have met
3 will start / **6** go
starts

6

Sample answer

Hi Max,

I'm going to a water park next Saturday. Would you like to come? My friend Paul is coming too. He went there last month and loved it. We can get there by train. I think it will be amazing!

Stan

Use linking words and relative pronouns to make longer sentences

1

10 sentences

2

Dan woke up <u>and</u> got out of bed. He didn't look at his clock. He opened the fridge, <u>but</u> it was almost empty. He was hungry, so he decided to go out for some food. He went to a café, <u>but</u> it was closed <u>because</u> it was only 6.30 in the morning!

3

1 but
2 and
3 so
4 because
5 but
6 so

4

1	which	**3**	who
2	who	**4**	which

5

1	who	**2**	which

6

1	who	**3**	which
2	which	**4**	who

Reading and Writing Part 6: A short message

1

Write about three things. Write 25 words or more.

2

1	don't	**3**	Shall	**5**	Why
2	could	**4**	Let's		

3

1	c	**3**	d	**5**	b
2	a	**4**	e		

4

2 I'm afraid I can't come to your party.

3 I'm sorry, but I'll be a bit late.

4 Guess what! I won the competition!

5

Hi Joe,

My cousin Beth is coming to visit on Saturday, and I <u>am</u> (I'm) really excited. <u>She is</u> (She's) very good at computer games <u>I have</u> (I've) got a new game and <u>we are</u> (we're) going to play some games together. Do you want to come too? <u>I will</u> (I'll) call you later.

Sam

6

You should say that you can't go to the concert, give a reason why you can't go and suggest another time when you can go

8

Sample answer

Hi Laura,

I'm sorry, but I can't go to the concert on Saturday. I have to stay at home because my grandparents are coming to visit. Why don't we meet on Sunday and go to the cinema?

See you soon,

Ana

Reading and Writing Part 7: A story

1

35 words or more

2

1	was feeling	**4**	was carrying
2	was raining	**5**	ate
3	arrived	**6**	played

3

1	First	**4**	Suddenly
2	Next	**5**	Then
3	Finally	**6**	Finally

4

1	tall	**4**	quick
2	empty	**5**	high
3	pleased	**6**	ready

6

Alice wanted to watch TV, but her TV was broken. She told her mum. They looked on their computer and quickly found a big, new TV online. It wasn't expensive, so Alice's mum bought it. The next day, the new TV arrived, and Alice felt really happy.

Speaking bank answer key

Giving personal information

1

	Paul	Lucia
Age	13	14
From	Madrid	Milan

2 1 b 2 c 3 d 4 a

🔊 46

Pablo: Hello. My name's Pablo and I'm 13 years old. I'm Spanish and I come from Madrid.

Lucia: Hi. My name's Lucia. I'm fourteen years old, and I'm Italian. I live in Milan.

Talking about habits, likes and dislikes

1 doing homework, meeting friends, playing tennis, watching TV

2 1 always get up 2 'm never 3 usually do 4 often watch 5 on Saturdays 6 sometimes mee

🔊 47

Girl: I always get up early on school days, and I'm never late for school. I usually do my homework when I get home from school. I don't often watch TV. I usually play tennis on Saturdays, and I sometimes meet my friends at the weekend too.

3 basketball

4 1 like 2 don't 3 listening 4 prefer 5 favourite

🔊 48

Boy: I like maths and science, but I don't like art. I enjoy listening to music, but I don't like singing because I'm not a very good singer. I love sport! I like tennis, but I prefer football to tennis. Basketball is my favourite sport because it's very exciting.

Giving opinions and reasons

1 cycling

2 1 Do 2 do 3 about 4 don't 5 think 6 going 7 What 8 prefer 9 fun 10 love

🔊 49

Girl: Do you like swimming?

Boy: Yes, I do. It's fun. What about you?

Girl: No, I don't like swimming. I think it's boring. But I love going to the cinema. It's really interesting. What do you think?

Boy: No, I think going to the cinema is expensive. I prefer to watch films at home. My favourite activity is cycling. Do you think cycling is fun?

Girl: Yes, I do. I love cycling!

3 1 b 2 a 3 a

🔊 50

1
Boy: I often travel to other countries with my family. I like travelling because you visit interesting places and you learn about different countries.

2
Girl: My brother loves skateboarding, but I don't like it because I think it's dangerous. You can fall down and hurt yourself.

3
Boy: This is my new computer game. I play it a lot. I'm not very good at it, but I love it because it's exciting. Oh, no!

4

🔊 51

1
Girl: I like reading because it's relaxing and you can learn about a lot of different things.

2
Boy: I love football because it's an exciting game, and you feel really good when you win.

3
Boy: I don't like shopping because there aren't any good shops here.

Agreeing and disagreeing

1 1

2 1 not sure about 2 That's true 3 agree with you 4 Yes, but

🔊 52

Girl: Do you play any musical instruments?

Boy: Yes, I'm learning to play the guitar. What about you?

Girl: I'm learning the piano. I think it's very difficult to learn an instrument.

Boy: I'm not sure about that. The guitar isn't very difficult, but it's important to practise every day.

Girl: That's true. I agree with you that it's important to practise so that you can get better. I think that lessons are very expensive, too.

Boy: Yes, but you can watch lessons online and teach yourself. That isn't expensive.

Dealing with problems

1   **1** Could you repeat   **2** Can you repeat   **3** say that again

2   **1** Could you repeat that again, please?
     2 Could you say that again, please?
     3 Can you repeat me the question, please?

🔊 **53**

1

Teacher:	Don't forget the school trip tomorrow. We're meeting at 9.45.
Girl:	Could you repeat that, please?
Teacher:	Yes. It's 9.45 tomorrow morning.
Girl:	Thank you.

2

Teacher:	Do you think swimming in the sea is dangerous?
Boy:	Can you repeat the question, please?
Teacher:	Of course. Do you think swimming in the sea is dangerous?
Boy:	Yes, I think that sometimes it can be dangerous, especially in bad weather.

3

Girl:	I'm glad you can come to my party. It's at my house. I live at 29, West Street.
Boy:	Could you say that again, please? I need to write it down.
Girl:	Sure. It's 29 West Street. It isn't far from here.

3   **1** c   **2** a   **3** b

4   **1** not, word   **2** what, called   **3** know, is

🔊 **54**

1

Boy:	I'm not sure what the word is, but you often play this on the beach, with your friends. You have a ball, and you hit the ball with your hand.

2

Girl:	I'm not sure what this is called, but it's something you wear around your neck in winter, when it's very cold.

3

Boy:	I don't know what the word is, but it's something you eat. It's sweet, and very cold, and you often eat it in the summer.

Speaking Part 1

1   Yes, she does.

2   **1** or   **2** because   **3** because

🔊 **55**

Examiner:	Now, let's talk about weekends. What do you do at weekends?
Ana:	I often go shopping, or I sometimes go to the cinema.
Examiner:	And who do you like spending your weekends with?
Ana:	I like spending my weekends with friends, because we laugh and have fun together.
Examiner:	Now, let's talk about shopping. Where do you like going shopping?
Ana:	I like going shopping in London because there are lots of good shops.
Examiner:	And what do you like buying?
Ana:	I like buying clothes and shoes because I'm interested in fashion.

4   **1** love   **2** buy   **3** bought   **4** liked   **5** 'm going to take

🔊 **56**

Examiner:	Now, please tell me something about presents that you buy for other people.
Ana:	Well, I love buying presents for people. I usually buy presents for people, when it's their birthday. For example, last month I bought a T-shirt for my brother and he really liked it. It's my friend's birthday next week, and I'm going to take her to the cinema as a present.

5   **1** b   **2** a   **3** b   **4** a   **5** b   **6** b

6   **1** have – present   **2** 'm going to meet – future
     3 watch - present   **4** cooked – past
     5 'm going to play – future   **6** bought - past

7   **1** c   **2** d   **3** e   **4** b   **5** a

🔊 **57**

Examiner:	Tell me something about what you like doing at home.
Ana:	I like watching films, and I enjoy playing video games. I've just got a new game, so I'm quite excited about that.
Examiner:	Tell me something about what you like to eat with friends.
Ana:	I sometimes go to restaurants with my friends, and I prefer Italian food. We went to a pizza restaurant last weekend, and it was very nice.
Examiner:	Tell me something about the clothes you like to buy.
Ana:	I love buying new clothes, and my favourite thing to buy is jeans, because I like wearing them. I bought some really nice jeans last week, so I was happy.
Examiner:	Tell me something about the places you like to visit.
Ana:	I don't like going to big cities because there's too much traffic. I like visiting places that are near the sea. I love swimming when the weather's hot.
Examiner:	Tell me something about the sports you like to do.
Ana:	I like playing football. I play for a team, and we have a game every Saturday. My team doesn't often win, but it's still fun.

Speaking Part 2

1 Yes, they do

Girl: So, do you like playing video games?

Boy: Yes, I do. I've got a lot of video games, and I often play with my friends. I think they're exciting. What do you think?

Girl: I'm not sure about that. I sometimes play video games, but I think they're a bit boring.

Boy: What about taking photos? Do you like taking photos?

Girl: I often take photos when I'm with my friends, but I don't have a camera. I take photos on my phone. What about you?

Boy: I like taking photos, too. I have got a camera, and I love taking photos of animals and the countryside.

Girl: What about cycling? I love cycling because it's fun, and it's healthy. I always go cycling at weekends. What do you think about it?

Boy: I agree with you that it's fun and it's also good exercise. What about music? Do you play any instruments?

Girl: No, I don't. But I enjoy listening to music. What about you? Do you play an instrument?

Boy: I'm learning to play the drums. I'd like to be in a band one day.

Girl: And what about reading books? Do you like reading?

Boy: Yes, I like reading books, for example adventure books. But I prefer films to books.

Girl: Yes, I agree with you. I think films are more exciting than books.

2 Yes, she does.

Examiner: So, which of these hobbies do you like best?

Girl: I like cycling the best because I enjoy being active and I like spending time outside, and I think that cycling keeps you fit and healthy.

3 1 think 2 sure 3 like 4 about 5 do 6 agree

Boy: I think video games are exciting. What do you think?

Girl: I'm not sure about that.

Boy: What about taking photos? Do you like taking photos?

Girl: I often take photos when I'm with my friends.

Girl: I take photos on my phone. What about you?

Boy: I like taking photos, too. I've got a camera.

Girl: I always go cycling at weekends. What do you think about it?

Boy: I agree with you that it's fun.

4 1 d 2 a 3 e 4 b 5 c

5

Boy: Well, I love music festivals because I'm a music fan. I think they're great. What about you?

Girl: I agree with you. I like going to music festivals with my friends. And do you like going to the beach?

Boy: Yes, I do. I like swimming in the sea and playing football on the beach. What about you?

Girl: Yes, I agree. Going to the beach is fun, when the weather's hot. And what about walking in the mountains? I don't like that because it's really difficult. What do you think?

Boy: I'm not sure. I like it because you can see the beautiful countryside. I like camping, too, because it's fun and you're outside. Do you agree?

Girl: No, I don't agree. I hate camping because I prefer to sleep in a comfortable bed! But I like picnics. I often go for picnics with my friends in the summer. Do you like picnics?

Boy: Yes, I do. When it's sunny, it's lovely to eat outside in a nice place, for example near a river.

6

Examiner: Which of these activities do you like the best?

Student: I like going to music festivals because you can listen to some exciting bands and also spend time with your friends and have fun.

Examiner: Do you prefer to go on holiday to the beach or the countryside?

Student: I prefer to go to the beach because in the countryside it's sometimes a bit boring, because there aren't many people and there are no restaurants or cafés. At the beach there are lots of people, so it's more exciting.

Examiner: Do you prefer swimming in the sea or in a swimming pool?

Student: I prefer swimming in the sea. It's more interesting because you can see different things around you, but in the swimming pool you just have to go up and down all the time, so I think it's a bit boring.

Phrasal verb builder answer key

Getting about

1

get back = return
take off = leave the ground (a plane)
come round = visit someone's house
come in = enter a place
pick (someone) up = collect someone from somewhere

2

1 takes off   **2** get back   **3** picked (me) up
4 come in   **5** came round

In the morning

1

take something off = stop wearing
wake up = stop sleeping
get up = get out of bed
go out = leave
put something on = start wearing

2

1 wake up   **2** get up   **3** take off
4 put (my school uniform) on   **5** go out

People and communication

1

grow up = become an adult
call someone back = return a phone call
find out = get information about
look after = take care of
get on with someone = be friendly with someone

2

1 look after   **2** get on   **3** find out   **4** call (you) back
5 grew up

Other phrasal verbs

1

lie down = usually something you do before you go to sleep
turn off = stop a machine or light from working
fill in = write information on a form
give back = give something to the person who gave it to you
try on = put on clothes to see if they fit

2

1 lie down   **2** turn off   **3** try (shoes) on   **4** fill in
5 give back

Workbook answer key

Unit 1

Grammar

1

3 We've got / We have got six cousins.
4 Has she got an older sister? Yes, she has.
5 I haven't got / have not got a younger brother.
6 Harry's got / Harry has got very short fair hair.
7 Have your friends got nicknames? No, they haven't.
8 They haven't got / have not got their trainers with them.

2

2 I get – I've got / I have got
3 I got – I've got / I have got
4 I get – I've got / I have got
5 everyone got – everyone's got / everyone has got
6 We've to – We've got to / We have got to
7 haven't – hasn't / has not
8 I've – I've got / I have got

3

2 walks to school, doesn't walk to school
3 has lunch
4 does, doesn't do
5 watches
6 goes to bed

4

2 How   5 Who
3 What   6 When
4 Where

5

Sample answers

2 I walk to school. / I go to school by bus. / I cycle to school.
3 I have toast and cereal. / I have cheese and ham.
4 My school is near my house.
5 My best friend is Sophia.
6 My next school holiday starts in July.

Vocabulary

1

2 daughter, son
3 Uncle, wife
4 children, cousins

5 husband
6 father
7 grandmother

3

2 wake up
3 walk to school
4 get home
5 do, homework
6 watch TV
7 go to bed

Reading and Writing Part 2

1 C   5 B
2 B   6 A
3 C   7 C
4 A

Reading and Writing Part 7

Sample answer

One day, a boy was walking to school and it started to rain. He looked at the sky and saw a big, black cloud. He ran as fast as he could to school. He got to school, went to his classroom and looked out of the window. It was raining a lot. He was glad he was inside. [58 words]

Listening Part 3

1 B   4 B
2 A   5 A
3 C

Unit 2

Grammar

1

2 Danny has band practice every day except Sunday.
3 Danny often goes to school in his dad's car.
4 Danny visits his grandfather on Sundays.
5 Danny has swimming club twice a week.
6 Danny never goes to art club.

2

2 We have gone to the beach **every day**.
3 First we eat salad, **sometimes with** tomatoes, carrots and garlic.
4 She **always** likes to study.
5 On holiday I **often** eat it. / **I often eat it on holiday.**
6 My son is sick **every day**.
7 I **always** drink juice.

3

2 do you like
3 'd like / would like
4 Would you like
5 'd like / would like
6 Do you like
7 like
8 'd like / would like

Vocabulary

1

1 F   3 E   5 B
2 C   4 D   6 A

2

2 good at   5 terrible at
3 doesn't like   6 prefers
4 enjoy   7 interested in

3

Sample answers

1 I love / hate / don't like / enjoy cooking.
2 I love / hate / don't like / enjoy singing.
3 I'm good / bad / terrible at dancing.
4 I'm (not) interested in science.
5 I (don't) enjoy / (don't) like / hate / love spending time with my family.
6 I (don't) enjoy / (don't) like / hate / love going to the countryside and learning about nature.

Reading and Writing Part 3

1 B   4 A
2 C   5 B
3 C

Listening Part 4

1 C   4 B
2 C   5 A
3 B

Reading and Writing Part 5

1 of   4 them
2 when/if   5 who
3 to   6 What

Unit 3

Grammar

1

2 Are, any   6 isn't any
3 is some   7 are any
4 is, an   8 aren't any
5 isn't a

2

3 has to tidy
4 doesn't / does not have to tidy
5 have to make
6 has to wash
7 doesn't / does not have to wash
8 have to tidy
9 doesn't / does not have to clean
10 has to clean

Vocabulary

1

chair	fridge	shower
cooker	lamp	sofa
cupboard	mirror	stairs
desk	shelf	toilet

S	O	F	A	C	H	A	I	R
			O	L	F			S
C	U	P	B	O	A	R	D	H
S			K	M	I	E	E	
T			E	P	D	S	L	
A			R		G	K	F	
I		S	H	O	W	E	R	
R	T	O	I	L	E	T		
S			M	I	R	R	O	R

2

2 bathroom
3 living room / sitting room
4 bedroom
5 kitchen

3

A	cheese	E	fish
B	egg	F	salad
C	bread	G	burger
D	chicken	H	potatoes

4

1 chicken, burger
2 onion, potato / potatoes
3 fish
4 juice
5 omelette
6 jam
7 rice
8 cheese
9 bread
10 salad

5

Sample answers

1 I usually eat eggs and bread for breakfast.
2 I have lunch in the canteen at school.
3 My favourite food is chicken and my favourite drink is orange juice.
4 I sometimes cook at home.
5 I only eat in a restaurant on special days. For example, I eat in a restaurant when it's someone's birthday.

Reading and Writing Part 4

| 1 | B | 3 | C | 5 | C |
| 2 | A | 4 | B | 6 | A |

Listening Part 2

1 vegetables
2 Whiteside
3 0996 548013
4 Monday(s)
5 5.15 / (a) quarter past five

Reading and Writing Part 7
Sample answer

A boy is looking in the fridge. There is a roast chicken, some cheese and some eggs. He puts some bread and some chicken into a box. Then he goes to the forest and meets his friends. They are having a picnic. [42 words]

Unit 4

Grammar

1

2 are you going
3 aren't going / are not going / 're not going
4 are going / 're going
5 is moving / 's moving
6 are you doing
7 am waiting / 'm waiting
8 am going / 'm going

2

2 She isn't / is not / 's not eating.
3 She isn't / is not / 's not drinking (anything / (her/the) water).
4 She is / 's wearing (trainers, (sports) trousers and a T-shirt / sports clothes).
5 She isn't / is not / 's not sitting.
6 She is / 's holding a bottle (of water).
7 She is / 's running.

3

2 practise
3 is / 's, doing
4 does not / doesn't want
5 'm / am playing
6 play
7 'm / am not doing
8 does, have
9 'm / am writing

Vocabulary

1

2 go swimming
3 play basketball
4 go skateboarding
5 play volleyball
6 go cycling
7 go ice skating
8 go surfing
9 play football

2

a	basketball	f	volleyball
b	skateboarding	g	swimming
c	surfing	h	football
d	cycling	i	ice skating
e	skiing		

3

2	golf	5	martial arts
3	ice hockey	6	aerobics
4	table tennis		

4

1	comfortable	4	fun
2	cheap	5	bright
3	warm	6	pretty

Listening Part 1

1	A	4	B
2	C	5	C
3	B		

Reading and Writing Part 1

1	B	4	C
2	A	5	B
3	B	6	A

Reading and Writing Part 6
Sample answer

Hi, Ali

My nearest sports centre is in my village, next to the park. You can play badminton, squash and volleyball there and it's got a swimming pool. I never go because I don't like sports!

Bye, [37 words including greetings]

Unit 5

Grammar

1

2	drank	6	started
3	ate	7	found
4	enjoyed	8	opened
5	tried	9	went

2

2	was	7	were
3	started	8	invited
4	didn't / did not stop	9	had
5	didn't / did not do	10	didn't / did not mind
6	didn't / did not sleep	11	played
		12	didn't / did not hear

4

Sample answers

2 When were you born?
   I was born (in 2004 / on 28th July 2004).

3 What time did you get up this morning?
   I got up at (6 am).

4 Where did you go last weekend?
   I went (to the beach).

5 What did you have for breakfast today?
   I had cereal.

5

1	ago	4	in
2	at	5	on
3	on	6	in

Vocabulary

1

1	e	4	b
2	a	5	f
3	c	6	d

2

1	e	4	f
2	d	5	a
3	c	6	b

3

2 department store
3 newsagent
4 university
5 bank
6 police station
7 cinema
8 sports centre
9 online shop
10 bookshop

4

2 3/8/1492 – Columbus set out on his first voyage to America.

3 10/3/1876 – Alexander Graham Bell made the first telephone call.

4 4/7/1776 – The United States of America declared independence from Britain.

5 17/12/1903 – The Wright brothers made the first powered aeroplane flight.

6 20/7/1969 – Man first landed on the moon.

Reading and Writing Part 2

1	B	5	C
2	C	6	A
3	B	7	A
4	A		

Listening Part 2

1

1 Scoresound
2 25th November / 25/11
3 clothes
4 a (free) poster
5 5.75

2

Sample answers

1 What's the address (of the museum)?
   (It's in) Victoria Square, Branton.

2 What's the name of the exhibition?
   (It's called) Scoresound.

3 When does/will the exhibition end?
   (It ends on) 25th November / November 25.

4 What's in the new fashion room?
   (There are) clothes worn by famous pop stars (over the last 50 years).

5 What does the entrance ticket include?
   (It includes) a free poster.

6 How much does it cost for teenagers?
   (It costs) £5.75.

Reading and Writing Part 6
Sample answer

Hi, Sam
I went to Marley's department store yesterday. I went there because I wanted to buy a notebook and some pens. It is really big. It has three floors of clothes, and furniture and other things for the home on two more floors. It's a nice place. I really liked the café on the first floor.
Bye!
Fred [55 words, not including salutations]

Unit 6
Grammar

1

1	faster	4	busier
2	slower	5	more expensive
3	bigger	6	cheaper

2

2 the most big   the biggest
3 the bests football players   the best football players
4 the goodest group   the best group
5 the bigest room   the biggest room
6 the last technology   the latest technology
7 the more beautiful dress   the most beautiful dress
8 best my bedroom   my bedroom best

3

3 Journey A is further/farther than journey C.
4 Journey B is the longest.
5 Journey A is cheaper than journey B.
6 Journey B is the most expensive.
7 Train B is older than train C.
8 Train C is the newest.

Vocabulary

1

2	B, C	6	B, C, F
3	A, C	7	B, F
4	E, F	8	B, C, F
5	B, C	9	A, C

2

1	Ships	4	helicopter
2	coach	5	motorbike
3	underground	6	Lorries

3

2	walk	5	ride
3	fly	6	sail
4	drive		

4

Girl's answers

1 by train
2 by car
3 Manchester airport
4 No, they can't.
5 my uncle
6 I don't know. (Boy says: *About three months.*)

5

1	a roundabout	3	traffic lights
2	a bridge	4	a crossing

Reading and Writing Part 3

1	B	4	C
2	C	5	B
3	B		

Listening Part 5

1	B	4	G
2	A	5	D
3	C		

Reading and Writing Part 5

1	we	4	the
2	Do	5	by
3	than	6	on

Unit 7

Grammar

1

2 mustn't listen   **7** mustn't talk
3 must drink   **8** must show
4 must take   **9** mustn't ride
5 mustn't use   **10** mustn't play
6 mustn't eat

2

Sample answers

You mustn't talk.
You mustn't eat.
You must be quiet.
You must turn your mobile phone off.

3

1 d   **4** f
2 a   **5** e
3 c   **6** b

5

Sample answers

2 Paul wants to wake up earlier. He shouldn't go to bed so late.
3 Georgio wants to learn Spanish. He should watch Spanish TV.
4 Deniz wants to read more. She should get some good books from the library.
5 Selina wants to eat better food. She shouldn't eat chips and burgers too often.
6 Ben wants to meet some new people. He should join a club.

6

4 Zara could cook vegetable soup in 2015.
5 Zara could ride a bike in 2010.
6 Zara can swim now.
7 Zara couldn't understand 100 English words in 2005.
8 Zara couldn't play the piano in 2006.

7

1 well   **5** quietly
2 quickly   **6** comfortable
3 terrible   **7** happily
4 slowly

Vocabulary

1

1 science   **4** geography
2 maths   **5** history
3 art   **6** music

2

2 studies   **5** missed
3 teaches   **6** passed
4 spends

4

2 guitar, d   **4** keyboard, b
3 violin, a   **5** piano, e

Reading and Writing Part 1

1 B   **4** C
2 B   **5** C
3 A   **6** B

Listening Part 2

1 guitar   **4** *Improve*
2 Wednesday(s)   **5** 23.20
3 58

Reading and Writing Part 6

1

1 opening and closing language
2 Next week I'm going to an interesting place near your town. I really like it there. The place is near the lake and it has a café. I like looking around it because it is very interesting. Usually, there are a lot of people singing and dancing. It's great. I like it there because it's very interesting.

2

Sample answer

Hi, Nicky
In our music lessons, we sometimes sing and we sometimes play the keyboard. I'd love to learn to play the drums. I often listen to music at home, and I sometimes go to concerts.
Bye,
[35 words]

Unit 8

Grammar

1

2 He was sleeping.
3 They were singing.
4 They were talking / chatting / having/drinking coffee.
5 They were laughing.
6 She was studying.
7 *Student's own answer*

2

2 He wasn't dancing.
3 They weren't studying.
4 They weren't singing.
5 They weren't drinking coffee.
6 She wasn't laughing.
7 I wasn't doing an exam.

3

1 didn't stop, was watching
2 fell, was putting
3 saw, were walking
4 broke, was trying

5 was playing, didn't hear
6 built, were camping

Vocabulary

1

1 b   **3** d
2 a   **4** c

2

2 speak   **5** explore
3 visit   **6** try
4 learn

3

2 interesting   **5** exciting
3 tiring   **6** funny
4 boring   **7** amazing

Listening Part 5

1 A   **4** G
2 B   **5** F
3 C

Reading and Writing Part 4

1 B   **4** B
2 A   **5** A
3 A   **6** C

Reading and Writing Part 7

Sample answer

Olivia packed her football for a camping holiday with her dad. He wanted to go walking in the mountains, but Olivia wasn't interested. When they arrived at the campsite, they met Olivia's friends and their dad. Olivia played football with her friends, while their dads went walking. Everyone was happy!
[50 words]

Unit 9

Grammar

1

2 f   **5** g
3 a   **6** e
4 b   **7** d

3

2 Are you going to get up early tomorrow?
3 Is it going to rain?
4 Is he going (to go) to Portugal?*
5 Are you going to do lots of practice this week?
6 Is it going to stop soon?
7 Are we going to have dinner soon?
* It is common to use *going* instead of *going to go.*

4

2 to take   **5** writing
3 showing   **6** practising
4 to find   **7** sitting

Vocabulary

1

2	play	5	disco/dance
3	concert	6	exhibition
4	circus	7	party

2

1	a quiz show	4	the news
2	a cartoon	5	the weather
3	a music programme	6	a sports programme

3

2	artist	5	photographer
3	musician	6	guitarist
4	writer	7	actor

4

1	guitarist	4	artist
2	singer	5	actor
3	drummer	6	dancer

Reading and Writing Part 3

1	B	4	C
2	B	5	B
3	A		

Listening Part 4

1	B	4	A
2	B	5	A
3	C		

Reading and Writing Part 6

Sample answer

Hi, Paddy
I'm sorry, I can't come to the cinema with you on Wednesday because I'm going to visit my grandma. Can we go on Friday instead? I'd like to see 'Snow Flight'.
Harry
[31 words, not including salutations]

Unit 10
Grammar

1

2	may	5	will
3	won't	6	won't
4	may		

2

2 goes, will/'ll need
3 takes, will not / won't need
4 cycles, will/'ll feel
5 sees, will/'ll take
6 will/'ll put, starts
7 will not / won't take, is/'s

4

2 I am tired I'll / I will be tired
3 we would go we'll / we will go
4 I am going I'll / I will go
5 when you'll arrive when you arrive
6 you would not find it you won't / will not find it

Vocabulary

1

2	on a river	6	on a hill
3	in a field	7	in a wood
4	on a path	8	on a lake
5	by a gate		

2

1	summer	5	summer
2	winter	6	winter
3	autumn	7	spring
4	spring	8	winter

3

1	ice	5	cloud
2	wind	6	thunderstorm
3	rain	7	sun
4	fog	8	snow

Reading and Writing Part 7

Sample answer

Jack and Martin are going to play in the snow. They are wearing warm hats, jackets, boots and scarves. They take their dog on the path. It is snowing. They build a snow dog and give it a scarf. Their dog likes it, too!
[44 words]

Listening Part 1

1	B	4	A
2	A	5	B
3	C		

Reading and Writing Part 1

1	C	4	C
2	B	5	A
3	B	6	C

Unit 11
Grammar

1

2	flown	7	been
3	taken	8	done
4	caught	9	heard
5	forgotten	10	eaten
6	seen		

2

2	just	4	already
3	already	5	yet

4

2 has/'s, won
3 haven't / have not had
4 have/'ve, read
5 have/'ve, sat
6 hasn't / has not finished
7 has/'s, drunk
8 have/'ve, eaten
9 have/'ve, run

5

2 He's / He has been a waiter since 2016. He's / He has been a waiter for three years.
3 The cat hasn't / has not eaten anything since Tuesday.
  The cat hasn't / has not eaten anything for two days.
4 We've / We have lived in this house for 10 years.
  We've / We have lived in this house since 2009.
5 I've / I have had this bike since I was 12 years old.
  I've / I have had this bike for five years.
6 She's / She has been in the shop for an hour.
  She's / She has been in the shop since three o'clock.
7 They haven't / have not spoken to each other since last Sunday.
  They haven't / have not spoken to each for six days.

Vocabulary

1

2	mouth	9	hair
3	hands	10	back
4	tooth	11	foot
5	arms	12	nose
6	face	13	ears
7	eyes	14	neck
8	stomach		

2

1	c	5	b
2	d	6	e
3	f	7	h
4	a	8	g

3

+ feelings ☺	− feelings ☹
glad	*afraid*
great	angry
happy	bored
	sick
	sorry
	unhappy

4

2	bored	5	angry
3	sick	6	tired
4	afraid		

Reading and Writing Part 4

1	B	4	B
2	C	5	A
3	A	6	C

Listening Part 3

1	B	4	B
2	A	5	C
3	B		

Reading and Writing Part 2

1	C	5	C
2	B	6	B
3	A	7	A
4	C		

Unit 12

Grammar

1

2	are put	5	are started
3	is visited	6	are seen
4	is used	7	are spent

2

2 The first digital cameras were sold by a company called Logitech.

3 The first fridge was built by Jacob Perkins in 1834.

4 The first computer mouse was made of wood.

5 The first hairdryer was used by a French hairdresser.

6 The first text messages were written on 3rd December, 1992.

4

2 a is given b took
  b gives 4 a asks
3 a was taken b is asked

5

2 I think biology is as interesting as physics.

3 Mobile phone screens are not as big as tablet screens.

4 Lessons at school are not as much fun as school trips.

5 My dad's motorbike was as expensive as my mum's car!

6 My old bike was not as fast as my new bike.

Vocabulary

1

1 MP3 player
2 laptop
3 digital camera
4 keyboard
5 mobile phone/smartphone
6 mouse
7 screen
8 email
9 DVD player

2

2	email address	6	call
3	download	7	chat
4	text		
5	use		

3

1	e	5	c
2	b	6	d
3	f	7	a
4	g		

Listening Part 5

1	E	4	G
2	F	5	B
3	A		

Reading and Writing Part 5

1	has	4	Why
2	were	5	with
3	a	6	does

Reading and Writing Part 2

1	A	5	A
2	C	6	C
3	A	7	B
4	B		

Vocabulary extra

Unit 1 Vocabulary extra

1

2	d	5	c
3	e	6	f
4	a		

2

2 thirsty (The others are all physical characteristics.)

3 tired (The others all describe hair.)

4 bedroom (The others are all food.)

5 terrible (The others are all positive adjectives.)

6 yellow (The others are all hair colours.)

7 park (The others are all prepositions.)

8 surname (The others are all things you wear.)

Unit 2 Vocabulary extra

1

1	j	7	e
2	i	8	k
3	h	9	l
4	f	10	b
5	c	11	a
6	d	12	g

A 7 B 1 C 12 D 2 E 8 F 3

Unit 3 Vocabulary extra

1

1 balcony 2 steps 3 plants 4 wall
5 window 6 door 7 plant pot
8 lamp 9 roof 10 chimney

Unit 4 Vocabulary extra

1

1	g	5	d
2	b	6	h
3	f	7	e
4	c	8	a

A 4 B 5 C 8 D 7 E 3 F 6 G 1 H 2

Unit 5 Vocabulary extra

1

1	i	6	h
2	e	7	g
3	b	8	j
4	a	9	d
5	c	10	f

2

2 3/8/1492 Columbus set out on his first voyage to America.

3 10/3/1876 Alexander Graham Bell made the first telephone call.

4 4/7/1776 The United States of America declared independence from Britain.

5 17/12/1903 The Wright brothers made the first powered aeroplane flight.

6 20/7/1969 Man first landed on the moon.

Unit 6 Vocabulary extra

1

1	a car park	6	a crossing
2	a corner	7	a roundabout
3	a motorway	8	a square
4	traffic lights	9	a bridge
5	a road	10	a tunnel

Unit 7 Vocabulary extra

1

history	learning about past kings and queens	reading about things that happened hundreds of years ago
music	playing an instrument	singing
science	studying how plants grow	finding out about space
English	learning grammar	doing a listening test
geography	studying mountains and rivers	learning about weather in different countries
maths	adding numbers	learning how to find the size of a circle

Unit 8 Vocabulary extra

1

1 climbing		**4** having
2 visiting		**5** speaking
3 staying		**6** trying

2

2 awful		**5** great
3 dull		**6** brilliant
4 terrible		

Unit 9 Vocabulary extra

1

1 an exhibition		**4** a circus
2 a party		**5** a film
3 a concert		**6** a play

2

1 F		**4** T
2 T		**5** F
3 F		**6** F

Unit 10 Vocabulary extra

1

1 B **2** A **3** A/B **4** A/B **5** A **6** A
7 B **8** A/B **9** A

2

1 rainy		**4** clear
2 cool		**5** icy
3 Fine		

Unit 11 Vocabulary extra

1

1 F (You see with your eyes.)
2 T
3 T
4 T
5 F (People have one nose.)
6 T
7 F (Your feet are at the end of your legs. / Your neck is between your head and your body.)
8 T
9 F (You wear a hat on your head.)
10 F (People have two legs.)
11 T
12 F (You wear necklaces round your neck.)

2

1 appointment		**4** medicine
2 nurse		**5** ambulance
3 accident		

Unit 12 Vocabulary extra

1

open	visit	reply to	search for	upload	click on	
✓			✓	✓	✓	a file
✓	✓	✓				a web page
✓			✓	✓	✓	a video
✓		✓				a message
✓		✓			✓	an email
			✓			information

2 **Choose the correct adjective.**
1 busy **2** quicker **3** latest **4** broken **5** dead

Workbook audio scripts

🔊 **02** **Unit 1, Vocabulary, Exercise 2**

1
Joanna: My name's Joanna. I've got one brother, but I haven't got any sisters.

2
Joanna: I am my parents' only daughter. My brother, Oliver, is their only son.

3
Joanna: My Aunt Diana is married to my Uncle Jacob. Diana is Jacob's wife.

4
Joanna: Diana and Jacob have got two children – Ben and Joe. Ben and Joe are my cousins.

5
Joanna: My aunt Veronica hasn't got a husband – she doesn't want to get married yet.

6
Joanna: The two people with white hair are my mum's mother and father.

7
Joanna: My grandfather Jorge is one month younger than my grandmother.

🔊 **03** **Unit 1, Vocabulary, Exercise 4**

1
Girl: I start school at 9.00 every morning.
2
Girl: In the morning, I wake up at 7.00. Then I get out of bed.
3
Girl: I ride my bike to school, but my friend can walk to school because he lives very near.
4
Girl: I leave school on my bike at 3.00 p.m. and get home at 3.15 p.m. My mum is always there.
5
Girl: I'm a good student because I do my homework every day.
6
Girl: I like to watch TV with my family in the evening.
7
Girl: At night, I go to bed early because I need a lot of sleep.

🔊 **04** **Unit 1, Listening Part 3**

Mum: Kelly, I spoke to your singing teacher last night. You haven't got a lesson this week.
Kelly: OK, so when's my next lesson?
Mum: It'll be on the 15th of August – you're missing this week, which is the 8th of August, and on the 22nd of August, your teacher's away again.
Kelly: Right.
Mum: She said you need a new music book, too.
Kelly: Oh, OK. Where can we get that?
Mum: Well, they haven't got any music at the library, I've looked before. The bookshop's cheaper than the music shop, so we'll get it there.
Kelly: OK.
Mum: Which day shall we go?
Kelly: How about Thursday? You work late on Tuesdays and I've got dance club on Wednesday.

Mum: Fine.
Kelly: Will you pick me up after school?
Mum: No, I only finish work at quarter to four, so go home first. I'll see you there at four o'clock. Then we'll get to the shop about quarter past four.
Kelly: Right.
Mum: Would you like dinner in a restaurant afterwards?
Kelly: Yeah! I heard the burger restaurant's closed, but I'd like to go and have a pizza. The fish restaurant's a bit too far from the shops.
Mum: Great!

🔊 **05** **Unit 2, Grammar, Exercise 4**

Julian: Did you go to music club yesterday?
Peter: No, they played jazz and I don't like jazz much.
Julian: What kind of music do you like?
Peter: Rock, pop, classical – most kinds, but not jazz!
Julian: I'd like to come, too. Can I just come or do I have to ask the teacher first?
Peter: Just come when you want to. Would you like to come with me next week?
Julian: Yes, please. I'd like to join so I can learn to play an instrument.
Peter: Do you like all kinds of music?
Julian: I like modern music best, but I'd like to learn more about classical music and jazz, too.
Peter: Music club will be perfect for you!

🔊 **06** **Unit 2, Listening Part 4**

1 *You will hear two friends talking about going to art club. What do they say about going to the countryside to paint?*
Boy: It's Art Club today. Are you coming?
Girl: Yes – we're going outside to paint. I'm glad we are – it's fun doing that.
Boy: Absolutely. I really enjoyed it when we went to the city centre and painted outdoors in the town square.
Girl: Me too. And it will be interesting to paint the fields and the lake.
Boy: Yes, it will.

2 *You will hear a girl talking about a competition. What type of competition was it?*
Girl: I enjoyed the competition. I didn't win, but I played well and I didn't get too tired. But I missed a lot of balls. I wish I'd practised more – I need to hit the ball harder. A lot of the people I played were better than me, but they were older, too. I'll win more games when I'm older.

3 *You will hear a boy talking about joining a dance club. Why does he want to join the club?*
Boy: I'm joining the dance club this month. I always do loads of exercise, like playing basketball and swimming, but I'd like to do an activity I've never done before. At the club, they do dances from around the world, so I'll learn about all kinds of music too. I asked my friends to come along, but they're not interested.

4 *You will hear a girl, Kate, talking to a friend about films. What type of films does she like?*
Boy: What kind of films do you like, Kate?
Girl: Er… I like a few types… though not adventure films. They're a bit boring. Comedy films are too, I think, because nothing

exciting happens. And often, they're not even amusing. But you're never bored when you watch a horror film. They're great.

5 *You will hear two friends talking about a concert they went to. What did they think of the concert?*

Girl: Well, what did you think of the concert?

Boy: Not bad! Definitely better than the last concert we went to in that theatre.

Girl: Yes, that's true. That was awful. But it's always nice to go there – the sound quality is amazing. But they didn't play many songs, did they?

Boy: No. They only played for about an hour and a half which wasn't enough.

🔊 07 Unit 3, Grammar, Exercise 3

1
Man: Emily doesn't have to wash the dishes this week.
2
Man: Oliver has to wash the dishes this week.
3
Man: Emily has to tidy the living room this week.
4
Man: Oliver doesn't have to tidy the living room this week.
5
Man: Oliver and Emily both have to make their beds this week.
6
Man: Emily has to wash the kitchen floor this week.
7
Man: Oliver doesn't have to wash the kitchen floor this week.
8
Man: Oliver and Emily both have to tidy their bedrooms this week.
9
Man: Emily doesn't have to clean the bathroom this week.
10
Man: Oliver has to clean the bathroom this week.

🔊 08 Unit 3, Listening Part 2

Woman: Now, here's something interesting for all of you teenagers who are interested in TV programmes about food. A new show called *Chefs* is coming to your screens soon. It will include cooking and information about all kinds of subjects, such as healthy food and national dishes. In the first programme, young cooks tell us all about vegetables. They'll show us how to grow and cook them. But this won't be like a normal TV show: the programmes are not filmed in the TV centre. We're making the programmes at a school! It's called Whiteside School, that's spelt W-H-I-T-E-S-I-D-E. And we'd like you to call us with your ideas – we'll choose the best ones and then you can come and film with us! So phone us on 0996 548013. Now check your diary! This amazing new programme will be on Mondays. And on Tuesday evenings, you'll be able to chat to people from the show online. The first show's on 28th November, from five fifteen until five forty-five – write it down now!

🔊 09 Unit 4, Listening Part 1

1 *Where is Jessie playing table tennis?*

Girl: Where's Jessie, Robert? At the sports centre?

Boy: Well, she's playing table tennis with her friend, Kate, but not at the centre. They went to Kate's place after school.

Girl: To Kate's house, you mean?

Boy: That's right, and they're going to the sports centre to play volleyball after that.

2 *What does the girls' football team wear?*

Boy: Does your team wear black shirts, like ours?

Girl: With white numbers, yes. Our team wears nearly the same as yours, but our socks are white, not black.

Boy: Oh. So you wear white shorts, too?

Girl: We do, with a black number at the sides.

Boy: That sounds great!

3 *What time is Henry's skiing lesson?*

Man: Is your skiing lesson before or after mine this morning, Henry?

Boy: What time's yours, Dad? I can't remember.

Man: It's at 8.45.

Boy: Oh, well, mine starts half an hour later, at quarter past nine. You'll have to get up before me!

4 *What is the mother's gym teacher doing this evening?*

Boy: Why aren't you at your gym class this evening, Mum?

Woman: Our teacher can't do the class this week.

Boy: Is she ill again?

Woman: No, she's fine now. She's flying to Paris tonight because she's going to visit a friend there tomorrow.

Boy: She's lucky – I love flying!

5 *Where did Lily put the advertisement for her football ticket?*

Boy: Lily, hi. Did you sell that football match ticket that you don't want? I just heard someone on the radio asking for tickets.

Girl: Oh, I've sold mine. I put a poster up at my football club and someone there wanted it.

Boy: That's good.

Girl: Yes, Dad put an advertisement online first, but no one called us about that.

🔊 10 Unit 5, Grammar, Exercise 3

Man: Last summer, Simon went camping with his family near a castle in the mountains in Scotland. It was a beautiful place, but as soon as they arrived, it started to rain and it didn't stop for days! During the day, they didn't do any activities because it was too wet outside, and at night, they didn't sleep because the wind and the rain were so noisy. After four days of rain, the man who lived in the castle invited them to stay with him at the castle! After that, Simon and his family had a great time. They didn't mind the bad weather because they played games in the castle all day and they didn't hear the rain and the wind at night.

🔊 11 Unit 5, Listening Part 2

Woman: The Branton Museum of Pop Music is the city's most popular museum for visitors aged 12 to 18. Its new location in Victoria Square is much more central than its old Green Street address.

This month, it has a new exhibition called 'Scoresound', that's spelled S-C-O-R-E-S-O-U-N-D, and it explores film music, with hundreds of pictures, recordings and videos. It's open from the 31st of October until the 25th of November.

The museum's also just opened a new fashion room. Here, you can see the clothes worn by some of the most famous pop stars of the last 50 years.

You can travel to the museum by car or bus, and you get a free poster with your entrance ticket.

Museum tickets for adults cost eight pounds fifty, but for schoolchildren up to the age of 19 it's just five pounds seventy-five. However, children under five go free.

🔊 ⑫ Unit 6, Grammar, Exercise 4

1
Man: Journey A is shorter than journey B.
2
Man: Journey C is the shortest.
3
Man: Journey A is further than journey C.
4
Man: Journey B is the longest.
5
Man: Journey A is cheaper than journey B.
6
Man: Journey B is the most expensive.
7
Man: Train B is older than train C.
8
Man: Train C is the newest.

🔊 ⑬ Unit 6, Vocabulary, Exercise 3

1
Boy: How do you usually travel when you go on holiday?
Girl: We usually travel by train.
2
Boy: Do most students walk to your school or do they go by bus or car?
Girl: Most go by car!
3
Boy: Which airport do people in your town fly from?
Girl: They usually fly from Manchester airport.
4
Boy: Can 10-year-olds drive cars in your country?
Girl: No, of course they can't!
5
Boy: Does anyone in your family ride a motorbike?
Girl: Yes. My uncle rides one.
6
Boy: How long does it take for a ship to sail around the world?
Girl: I don't know. How long?
Boy: About three months, I think.

🔊 ⑭ Unit 6, Listening Part 5

Marcia: I'm going to start taking the school bus next week, Josh. Where should I catch it?
Josh: Well, I catch it from Hill Street. After the railway bridge, there's a roundabout, and my bus stop's there.
Marcia: OK. Does Max catch it there? He lives near you.
Josh: No. His mum drives him into town because she works at the motorbike shop. She leaves her car in the car park in George Street. Max catches the bus there.
Marcia: OK.
Josh: Oliver gets on at the bus stop in New Street, by the bridge – not the one near the cinema, the other one.
Marcia: Oh yes, I can catch it there, too. Who else goes on the bus?
Josh: Emily. She lives opposite the cinema, so she catches the bus there, not far from the tram stop.
Marcia: What about Katy, Emily's neighbour?
Josh: She doesn't like crossing the busy road, so she gets on the school bus next to the traffic lights behind the station.
Marcia: Oh yes.
Josh: Tom gets the bus too, at the crossing, near the supermarket.
Marcia: I know. Thanks, Josh.

🔊 ⑮ Unit 7, Grammar, Exercise 4

Girl: Jack is always hungry in the afternoon at school.
Boy: He should eat more at lunchtime.
Girl: Jack often forgets what his homework is.
Boy: He should write it down in a diary or notebook.
Girl: When it rains, Jack's clothes always get wet.
Boy: He should take an umbrella.
Girl: Jack wants to play tennis better.
Boy: He should take some lessons.
Girl: Jack is always tired in the morning.
Boy: He shouldn't go to bed late.
Girl: Jack's sister is angry with him.
Boy: He shouldn't borrow her things without asking.

🔊 ⑯ Unit 7, Vocabulary, Exercise 3

1
Boy: Hassan only has lessons at school in the morning.
2
Boy: Hassan studies 14 different subjects at school.
3
Boy: A man called Mr Ali teaches Hassan maths.
4
Boy: Hassan spends about two hours a night doing his homework.
5
Boy: Hassan only missed one day of school this year.
6
Boy: Hassan was very happy when he passed his exams last year.

🔊 ⑰ Unit 7, Listening Part 2

Woman: I'm here to tell you about my after-school music lessons here at Hilltop School. I'm Mrs Clarke. I know some of you can already play the violin because you learn it in music lessons at school. But if you'd like to try something else, you can learn to play the guitar with me. I have a class of ten students, and we have lots of fun! You have school band practice on Mondays, and then a free afternoon on Tuesdays. My lessons are on Wednesdays, starting at four o'clock and finishing at five thirty. We meet in the big room opposite Art Room 7 – it's Room 58. If you come, you must buy the book I use so you can practise at home. It's called *Improve* and you can buy it at Records, the music shop in the town centre. My lessons aren't expensive, because you learn in a group of ten. Each student pays just £23.20 a month, so it's about £5.80 a week. OK? Any questions?

🔊 ⑱ Unit 8, Grammar, Exercise 3

1
Man: He didn't stop laughing while he was watching the cartoon.
2
Man: The bowl fell on her foot while she was putting fruit in it.
3
Man: They saw the circus lorries in the street while they were walking to school.
4
Man: He broke the light on his bike while he was trying to repair the wheel.
5
Man: She was playing a computer game, so she didn't hear the phone.
6
Man: We built a fire for the first time while we were camping.

🔊 **19** **Unit 8, Listening Part 5**

Matthew: How was your holiday, Alice?
Alice: Great, thanks, Matthew. My course was really interesting.
Matthew: What did you learn?
Alice: How to write stories and news articles.
Matthew: Really? That sounds interesting.
Alice: Ahmet did a course, too. He learned how to prepare Chinese dishes on holiday – he wants to work as a food writer when he leaves school.
Matthew: Zena went to the same holiday camp, didn't she?
Alice: Yes, but she didn't need to do lots of reading and writing for her course. She had a week of Spanish dancing lessons.
Matthew: What about Zena's sister, Leah?
Alice: She learned to work with silver and made a beautiful necklace and earrings. I saw them yesterday.
Matthew: That's amazing! Is Mick still on holiday?
Alice: No, he had to come home on Monday to do a music exam. But before that, he did a windsurfing and sailing course at Lake Jarvis.
Matthew: Cool! When does Ellie come home?
Alice: Next week. She's doing a short course on biology this week. It's all about water plants and she loves it.
Matthew: Really?

🔊 **20** **Unit 9, Grammar, Exercise 2**

1
Man: She's putting her violin in its case because she's going to have a music lesson.
2
Man: He's studying hard because he's going to do an exam tomorrow.
3
Man: He's phoning his mum from school because he isn't going to go home for dinner.
4
Man: He's finding his seat in the theatre because the play is going to start soon.
5
Man: He's waiting in the street because a bus is going to come soon.
6
Man: She's putting her sweater in her bag because it is going to be cold this evening.
7
Man: He isn't enjoying the football match because his team isn't going to win.

🔊 **21** **Unit 9, Listening Part 4**

1 *You will hear a girl talking about a job she wants to do. What does she want to be?*
Girl: At school, I enjoy my art lessons, especially photography. My art teacher gave me some tips about taking great pictures on a trip to Kripps Lake. I also enjoy writing stories and finding out about people's lives. So I'd really like to put all those things together, and get a job on a newspaper or a magazine. But I don't think that'll be easy!
2 *You will hear Ravi talking to his dad. What are they discussing?*
Male: Haven't you got to do some maths exercises before dinner, Ravi? It's going to be ready in an hour.
Boy: I'll do them later, Dad – I want to watch a basketball game.
Male: You must do them before you watch TV.
Boy: OK. I'll do them now. I'll watch the game online after dinner.
Male: Fine.

3 *You will hear Holly talking about going to the library. Why is she going there?*
Girl: After my last lesson, I'm going to the school library. I need a book for my history research and they don't have it on the shelves – I checked online today. So I'm going to ask Mrs Stewart at the library to get it for me. She's really nice. I did this before, and the book arrived in about three days. I took it back yesterday.
4 *You will hear Rosie telling her mum about an exhibition. What was wrong with the exhibition?*
Woman: So why didn't you enjoy the exhibition, Rosie?
Girl: Well, Mum, there were lots of interesting paintings. I just wasn't sure what most of them were, or what they meant.
Woman: Oh. There are usually signs next to the pictures which tell you about them.
Girl: Not for this exhibition. There was just one poster, about the painter's life.
Woman: That's a pity.
5 *You will hear a boy talking to his mum about lunch. What is he going to make for lunch?*
Boy: I'm going to make lunch for us, Mum. There are lots of vegetables in the fridge – I'll cut them into little pieces and heat them in a pan with some water and some tomatoes, and lots of pepper and salt… and perhaps a bit of pasta. Then we'll have a nice hot bowl of it with some bread. OK?
Woman: Sounds lovely!

🔊 **22** **Unit 10, Grammar, Exercise 3**

1
Man: She'll go to the lake with Nick if he doesn't have football practice.
2
Man: If she goes to the lake, she'll need her swimming costume.
3
Man: If she takes a picnic, she won't need to buy food in the café.
4
Man: If she cycles around the lake, she'll feel tired.
5
Man: If she sees some interesting animals, she'll take photos of them.
6
Man She'll put her camera in her bag if it starts to rain.
7
Man: She won't take her umbrella if the weather's good.

🔊 **23** **Unit 10, Listening Part 1**

1 *What was the weather like last winter?*
Boy: Look at the snow outside, Daisy!
Daisy: Wow! We can go skiing this weekend – brilliant! We didn't ski last winter at all, did we?
Boy: No, it was too wet. But there may be a lot of ice on the roads this weekend, so we may not go skiing.
Daisy: Never mind.
2 *Who will go for the birthday meal with Jade and her parents?*
Mum: Who's coming to the restaurant with us on your birthday, Jade?
Jade: I asked three of my best friends, Mary, Kate and Emma, but Emma can't come.
Mum: OK … and of course your brother will be with us.
Jade: Yes, and you and dad.
Mum: Of course! We're looking forward to it!
3 *What happened during the storm last week?*
Boy: That storm was terrible last week, wasn't it?
Girl: Yes! A tree fell across the river and the water came up onto the road near our school.
Boy: Was the school OK?
Girl: Yes, but we had to walk there every morning until the

water went away. Cars couldn't get to the school, but it was OK on foot.

4 What does Eleanor do on the farm at weekends?

Eleanor: I usually go to my uncle's farm at weekends.

Man: Really? Where's the farm, Eleanor?

Eleanor: It's the one next to the horse-riding school.

Man: Cool! And you told me that he has lots of chickens – do you collect their eggs?

Eleanor: I do, and my friend Sue sells them in the farm shop. It's really good fun.

5 Where is Charlie's phone?

Girl: Why are you using my phone, Charlie?

Charlie: Because mine's in Mum's car and she's gone to see Grandma.

Girl: Are you sure? I saw it in the kitchen this morning.

Charlie: I know, but I went to the library after that. Mum drove me home, and she's just texted Dad to say she found it on one of the seats.

🔊 24 Unit 11, Grammar, Exercise 3

Dad: Hi, Adam. What are you doing? Have you had dinner yet?

Adam: No, I've just got home from my music lesson.

Dad: Oh, are you hungry?

Adam: Yes, I am. Do you want me to help you cook?

Dad: No, I've already done it. I made some fish soup earlier this evening, so it's all ready.

Adam: Great! Let's eat. I'll lay the table.

Dad: I've already done that too. But I haven't put any water or glasses on the table yet. Can you do that, please?

Adam: OK.

🔊 25 Unit 11, Listening Part 3

Christina: Hello, Leo.

Leo: What's the matter, Christina?

Christina: I've hurt my back, Leo.

Leo: Oh no! Have you seen the doctor?

Christina: Not yet. But I'm going to.

Leo: This morning?

Christina: No, I couldn't get an appointment – I'm going tomorrow afternoon. So I won't be at school until Thursday.

Leo: How did you do it?

Christina: Well, I walked home after basketball practice yesterday, and then it happened when I was going upstairs to the flat.

Leo: Really? So where are you now?

Christina: At home, lying down. Not on my bed, in the living room, on the sofa. Mum's here, making lunch in the kitchen.

Leo: So what activities can you do? You can't come skateboarding this evening, can you?

Christina: Mum says no, which I'm not pleased about. But swimming's OK – it may help. I'm not having my guitar lesson this evening, but that's fine!

Leo: Would you like something to read? I've got some good books about famous people.

Christina: OK – but I don't want to read about film actors. Maybe something about a pop star?

Leo: I've got nothing like that. There's one about a footballer – what about that?

Christina: Brilliant. Thanks, Leo.

🔊 26 Unit 12, Grammar, Exercise 3

1

Man: The first email was sent in 1971.

2

Man: The first digital cameras were sold by a company called Logitech.

3

Man: The first fridge was built by Jacob Perkins in 1834.

4

Man: The first computer mouse was made of wood.

5

Man: The first hairdryer was used by a French hairdresser.

6

Man: The first text messages were written on the third of December, 1992.

🔊 27 Unit 12, Listening Part 5

Woman: It's very quiet, Alice.

Girl: I know, Mum! Everyone's looking for something on the internet.

Woman: Even Dad?

Girl: Yes, he wants to download a movie – that one about the piano player.

Woman: Your brother wants to see that. What's *he* looking for?

Girl: He's looking for an electric guitar – he wants to start learning before our holiday.

Woman: I'll ask your sister to help him. What's she trying to find?

Girl: She's looking for a printer that'll work with her new tablet. … You know our cousin's here?

Woman: Really?

Girl: She was looking for a better tablet, but couldn't find one she wanted. Now she's searching for a digital camera to take on holiday.

Woman: Aunt Jane will be pleased.

Girl: Yes, she phoned earlier. She's looking on the internet because she wants a tablet that she saw on TV. That's for their holiday, too, so she can download pictures from her camera.

Woman: Can't you take pictures with a tablet? By the way, you know Grandma's going with them?

Girl: Yes. She says she needs a clock to travel with, so she's looking at a website now, then she's going to watch TV.

Woman: Right!

Acknowledgements

Author acknowledgements

Emma Heyderman would like to dedicate this book to her children, Sara and Alex; Jessica Smith would like to thank Roberto, Alex, Anna and Ethan.

Publishers acknowledgements

The authors and publishers are grateful and would like to extend a special thanks to Lorraine Poulter, Sarah Dev-Sherman (Project Manager – for holding everything together so brilliantly), Rob Vernon and Trish Chapman (Editors), and Wild Apple Design.

In addition, the publishers and authors would like to thank the following for their role in reviewing the material in general and in particular those who participated in the development of the exam tasks: Jane Coates, Sara Georgina Vargas Ochoa, Cressida Hicks, Annie Broadhead, Anthony Cosgrove, Sarah Dymond, Nicola Foufouti, Liz Gallivan, Joanna Kosta, Darren Longley, Lucy Mordini, Clare Nielsen-Marsh, Alison Sharpe, Ingrid Solberg, Sheila Thorne, Catriona Watson-Brown and Susan White.

Development of this publication has made use of the Cambridge English Corpus (CEC). The CEC is a computer database of contemporary spoken and written English, which currently stands at over one billion words. It includes British English, American English and other varieties of English. It also includes the Cambridge Learner corpus, developed in collaboration with the University of Cambridge ESOL examinations. Cambridge University Press has built up the CEC in order to provide evidence of authentic language use to better inform the production of learning materials.

This product is also informed by English Profile, a collaborative programme designed to enhance the learning, teaching and assessment of English worldwide. Its main partners are Cambridge University Press and Cambridge ESOL exams and its aim is create a profile for English usage based on the Common European Framework of Reference for Languages (CEFR). English Profile outcomes, such as the English Vocabulary Profile provide detailed information based on language level and help inform the language that learners can be expected to demonstrate at each CEFR level, offering a clear benchmark for learner's proficiency. For more information, please visit www.englishprofile.org.

The authors and publishers acknowledge the following sources of copyright material and are grateful for the permissions granted. While every effort has been made, it has not always been possible to identify the sources of all the material used, or to trace all copyright holders. If any omissions are brought to our notice, we will be happy to include the appropriate acknowledgements on reprinting and in the next update to the digital edition, as applicable.

Photography

The following images are sourced from Getty Images.

Front cover photography by Pawel Toczynski/Photographer's Choice/Getty Images; fitopardo.com/Moment/Getty Images; Laurie Noble/DigitalVision/Getty Images; Sir Francis Canker Photography/Moment/Getty Images; vladj55/iStock/Getty Images Plus/Getty Images; EnginKorkmaz/iStock Editorial/Getty Images Plus/Getty Images; Hero Images/Getty Images.

Illustration

Giuliano Aloisi from Advocate Art